For Marianna, Helen, Charmaine, Marie, Lil,
Mary Ellen, and Annie, who when I was drowning
in a car pool threw me a line ... always a funny one

Contents

Foreword

Soon after the West was settled, Americans became restless and began to look for new frontiers.

Bored with the conveniences of running water, electricity, central heating, rapid communication, and public transportation, they turned to a new challenge . . . the suburbs.

The suburbs were discovered quite by accident one day in the early 1940's by a Welcome-Wagon lady who was lost. As she stood in a mushy marshland, her sturdy Red Cross shoes sinking into the mire, she looked down, and exclaimed, "It's a septic tank. I've discovered the suburbs!"

News of the discovery of a septic tank spread and within weeks thirty million city dwellers readied their station wagons and began the long journey to the edge of town in search of a bath and a half and a tree.

It wasn't easy for the first settlers. They planted trees and crabgrass came up. They planted schools and taxes came up. Surveyors planted stakes and they disintegrated.

The first winter, more than half of the original settlers perished. Some lost their way in cul-de-sacs and winding streets with the same name trying to find their way home.

Other poor devils died of old age trying to merge onto the freeway to the city. One was attacked by a fast-growing evergreen that the builder planted near his front door. (They named a high school after him.)

There wasn't a day that went by that they weren't threatened by forces from the city: salesmen of storm doors, Tupperware and Avon ladies, traffic lights, encyclopedia salesmen, Girl Scout cookie pushers, and Golden Arches everywhere.

The survival by at least one family of PTAs, garage sales, car pools, horse privileges, Sunday drivers, Little Leagues, and lights from the shopping center is what this book is all about.

It traces the migration of the Bombeck family from their modest—but pathetic—apartment in the heart of the city to a plat house (one original and 216 carbons) just outside the city limits.

They make the trip with a son who has spoken

four words in five years ("I get the window"), their daughter who sleeps with a baton, and a toddler who has never known anything but apartment living and consequently does not own a pair of hard shoes.

It took a week to load their station wagon and after the good-byes they settled back to enjoy their new adventure.

"Look, honey, sit down on the seat. Daddy cannot drive with scissors in his ear. No, I don't know how long it has been since I cut the hairs in my ears! Erma, for God's sake, find something for him to do."

"Are we there yet?"

"It's my window and I say when it goes down and when it goes up. Mom! Isn't it *my* window?"

"You did not see a cow and if you mark it down I'm going to mark down a chariot on my list. A chariot gives me fifty points."

"I'm hungry."

"Start the motor. They'll be better when we get moving."

"Erma, do you smell something? Check the dog."

"The dog checks out."

"Check the feet of the kids."

"They all check."

"Check your own."

"You check yours first."

"Mom! I'm gonna be sick."

"You are not going to be sick and that's my final word!"

"Boys! Get your hands in this car or they'll blow off."

"How many kids had their hands blown off last year?"

"Too many to count."

"Did you ever see a hand that blew off on your windshield, Dad?"

"Erma, for God's sake find something for the kids to do."

"Mom! Andy took a bite out of a cookie and put it back. I'm telling."

"You tell about the cookies and I'm telling about your chicken bone collection."

"Stop the car! That's what we smell."

"Dad, when you get mad the veins in your nose swell up."

"I thought you were going to give them a sedative. How much farther?"

"We've got a hairpin, a thumbnail and a breath-mint to go, according to this map."

"Can't you interpret a simple road map?"

"Don't shout at me, Bill, I can't handle shouting today."

"I'm not shouting, I'm just suggesting that you are a high-school graduate and are capable of interpreting a simple scale on a map."

"Hey, Dad, I just saw a hand fly by."

"What day is it?" I asked. "I don't know how much longer I can stand the driving, the confinement, the loneliness. Not being able to talk to anyone. Bill, maybe we shouldn't have come."

"It won't be long now!" he said.

The Bombecks made it to the suburbs in their station wagon on June 9th. It was the longest fifty-five-minute drive any of them had ever endured.

CHAPTER ONE

Station Wagons . . . Ho!

Staking Out a Claim

It was either Thomas Jefferson—or maybe it was John Wayne—who once said, "Your foot will never get well as long as there is a horse standing on it."

It was logic like this that attracted thirty million settlers to the suburbs following World War II.

The suburbs were a wilderness with nothing to offer but wide, open spaces, virgin forests, and a cool breeze at night that made you breathe deep, close your eyes and sigh, "My God! Who's fertilizing with sheep dip?"

My husband held out against migration for as long as he could. Then one day we heard from our good friends, Marge and Ralph, who, together with their two children, set out in one of the first station wagons to a housing development thirty miles south of the city.

As Marge wrote, "We reached the suburbs on the 14th. There was no water and no electricity in our house so we had to hole up in a Holiday Motel for three days. The pool wasn't even heated.

"The yard is barren and there are no sidewalks. Mud is everywhere. There is no garbage pickup, our old stove won't fit in the new hole, and the general store has never heard of Oregano.

"We have aluminum foil at the windows to keep the sun from fading the children. I feel like a turkey. We have to claim our mail at the post office a mile and a half away. There is no super. We have our own washer and dryer which don't require quarters. I understand, however, that at the end of the month, there is something called a utility bill that is presented to us.

"There are some bright spots. We have a bath and a half. It is wonderful not to have to take numbers any more. Tomorrow, we are going to visit our first tree. It is situated on the only 'wooded' lot in

the subdivision and is owned by the builder's daughter. Pray for us. . . . Affectionately, Marge."

"Doesn't that sound exciting?" I said, jumping to my feet.

"You say the same thing when your soup is hot."

"Where's your adventurous spirit?" I asked. "It's a new world out there—full of challenges. We're young yet. We could survive."

He put down his paper and swept his arms around to encompass the entire apartment. "What! Move and give up all of this?"

I looked around. I had to iron in the playpen. The kids were stacked in a triple bunk at night like they were awaiting burial at sea. If the phone rang, I had to stand on my husband's face to answer it. The dog slept under the oven, next to the crackers. And one day I yawned, stretched my arms and someone stored the complete works of Dr. Seuss and a pot of African violets on them.

"You'd never survive," he predicted. "It's a raw frontier—no schools, no churches, and only three registered Republicans. Frankly, I don't think you have the stamina or the threshold of pain for it."

"Stamina!" I shouted. "Are you telling me I have no stamina? A woman who has lived on the fourth floor of this apartment building for five years with the stairs out of order has no stamina? I have legs

like a discus thrower. As for pain, I have been known to go without support stockings for as long as two hours."

"Do you honestly think you could move to a land where your mother is a 35-cent toll charge for the first three minutes?"

I hesitated, then squared my shoulders and said, "Yes!"

It was probably my imagination, but I thought I heard a whip crack and a voice shout, "Station Wagons . . . Ho!"

The selling of the suburbs made the coronation of Queen Elizabeth look like an impulse.

On a Sunday afternoon you could tour Cinderella's Red Coach Farms, Mortgage Mañana, Saul Lieberman's Bonsai Gardens, or Bonaparte's Retreat ("Live the Rest of Your Life Like a Weak King").

Every development had its gimmick: flags flying, billboards, free rain bonnets, balloons for the kiddies, and pom pom girls that spelled out LOW INTEREST RATES in script.

My husband spread out the newspaper and together we went over the plats we had visited.

"What did you think of Tahitian Village?" he asked.

"Cute," I said, "but a little overdone. I mean dropping the kids into a volcano to play each morning just . . ."

"What about Chateau on Waldren's Pond?"

"Call it a woman's intuition, but I've never trusted a lake that had a sudsing problem on Monday mornings."

"Wanta check out Sherwood Forest?"

"Why not?"

The sales office of Sherwood Forest was a tree stump surrounded by five or six salesmen dressed in tunics. Nearby was a plastic campfire that held a plastic pig on a spit and beyond that were 800 plastic houses.

"Welcome to Sherwood Forest," said a salesman schlepping along in a brown frock, a rope, and a pair of sandals. "I'm Friar Tuck and if you have any questions, feel free to ask them."

"If this is Sherwood Forest," I asked, "where are the trees?"

"You're standing over it," he said, staring at my knees.

My husband picked up the price list.

"You'll find that it is in keeping with the Robin Hood philosophy," he smiled.

We bolted toward the car, pursued by six Merry Men.

The adventure of moving to the suburbs had nearly worn off when we stumbled into Suburbian Gems.

"How much are the houses?" asked my husband.

"We have one standard price in Suburbian Gems," said the salesman. "$15,000."

We couldn't believe it. "Could we see the tracts?" we asked. He pulled down a giant map behind him solid with blocks representing houses. "I'm afraid we're pretty well sold out," he said. "The Diamond section went before we even advertised. Jade went fast. So did Ruby. And Pearl. I see even Zircon is blocked off."

"What's left?" we asked.

"Frankly Fake," he said. "Climb in the car and I'll drive you over to the sites so you can get the feel of the development."

When we pulled up in front of the house, I couldn't believe it. I got out of the car and ran through the two-story iron gates, up the half mile of driveway to the veranda porch, touched the massive white pillars and ran my fingers over the large carved door. "It's Tara!" I said, my eyes misting, "I've come home to Tara."

"You understand, this is only the model home," said the salesman.

I buried my face in the wisteria that crept along

the windows. "We understand. Could we see the rest of it?"

The double doors opened and our voices echoed our pleasure in the house, from the huge foyer to the curved stairway leading to the second floor.

Then, inside the living room, I saw it—the fireplace. A warmth came over me. I could see my husband standing against it in a sports coat with leather patches on the elbows holding a brandy and a copy of Emerson's essays.

I visualized me hanging a della Robbia wreath over it at Christmas and laughing children basking in its reflection after a snow. "We'll take it," I said suddenly.

As my husband lifted his hand to touch my face in a gesture of love, he was amazed to find a pen in it.

"If you will just sign the purchase agreement," said the salesman, " we can get on with the details of your new home in Frankly Fake."

I squeezed my husband's arm as he signed the agreement.

"We've never had a fireplace before."

"Oh, then you want the model with the fireplace?" asked the salesman.

We nodded.

"Well, now, is there anything else about the Williamsburg model that you like?"

"We like everything," I said.

"Oh, then you want the second floor, the extra baths, the tiled foyer, the stairway, the veranda porch, the larger lot . . . ?"

"Are you saying all those things are extra?"

"The Williamsburg is our best home," he said stiffly. "Our basic $15,000 is much the same only on a smaller scale."

"How small?" asked my husband.

"Let's see," he said, checking his price list. "The Pee Wee has three bedrooms and a one-car garage, spouting to protect your porch from the sun, full landscaping, and 850 luxurious square feet."

"Does it have a family room?"

"Two of them—both in white fixtures."

"But the Pee Wee does have the pillars and the porch . . ." I asked anxiously.

"I told you, it has everything except a second story, stairway, entranceway, and extra lot. Now, that covers about everything except what you want to do about the garage."

"What about the garage?" asked my husband.

"Do you plan on putting your car in it?"

"It crossed our minds."

"I see. I only mention it because a lot of people

like to have a driveway leading to it. You don't have to, you understand, but it does get a little muddy and it's worth the extra cost to some people to have it filled in."

"But everything else is included in the original price?" asked my husband.

"Absolutely. All you have to do is make some decisions regarding the quality of materials. For example, all wiring is borderline standard unless you want to pay extra and have it pass inspection. (We nodded.) I think that's wise. Now, about your tub. Do you want it hooked up under your shower?"

We nodded numbly.

"I assumed you did because you already said you wanted to put a car in your garage and that's where we usually store the tub until the owner tells us otherwise. Speaking of storage, you are aware that without the second story, there is a crawl space over your entire house for storage?"

We smiled happily.

"Do you have some way of getting up there or do you want us to install a pull-down stairway as an extra? Let's see—apart from the paint, floor covering, spouting, storm windows, kitchen hardware, countertops, lighting fixtures, and keys, which are all extra, I think that does it."

His fingers fairly raced across the keys of the

27

tabulator as the extras mounted. Finally, he smiled and said, "The final tab is $29,500. Welcome to Frankly Fake!"

As my husband handed back the pen, he smiled, waved it aside, and said, "Keep it. As a token of our mutual faith in one another."

Out of the corner of my eye, I saw him add, "Pen @ 59 cents" bringing the total to $29,500.59.

Lot No. 15436 . . . Where Are You?

We must have driven two and a half hours before we found our house.

"Are you sure this is it?" asked my husband.

"I'm sure," I said tiredly. "This is the eighth house from the corner and the builder always staggers his styles so they won't all look alike. I counted them. There were the Williamsburg, the Richmond, the Shenandoah, and the Pee Wee, a Williamsburg, a Richmond, a Shenandoah, and this is our Pee Wee."

"I thought it was supposed to look like Mt. Vernon," whined our daughter, "with big pillars."

"But it does have pillars," I said, pointing toward the four supports that looked like filter-tip cigarettes.

"Will they grow?" asked our son.

"Children, please!" said my husband. Then, turning to me he asked, "Happy?"

I looked at the packing boxes stacked at the curb, the mail box on the ground, chunks of plaster embedded in the mud, windows dusty and spackled with paint and said, "I wish I could tell you—in front of the children."

"Well, let's go in and get settled," he said. "And take your muddy boots on the porch inside."

"What muddy boots?" I said. "Aren't they yours?"

"They're mine," said a woman coming out of one of the bedrooms.

"Who are you?" asked my husband.

"I live here," she said.

"Isn't this 5425 Ho Hum Lane?" he asked.

"Yes, but it's 5425 Ho Hum Lane Northeast. It used to be 18 Bluebird of Happiness Drive, but then the other street came through and changed it. When we bought it, it was 157 Squirrel Road, but Ho Hum Lane is on a circle and the even numbers change to the odd numbers at the house where the door is on backwards. You know the one?"

"Right. That's two down from the chuckhole in the road where your car falls through."

"That's the one. Besides, 5425 isn't going to be

your permanent number. That's a lot number and will change when the post office assigns you your new one."

"Oh? Where's the post office? We haven't been able to find it."

"No one is quite sure yet. You notice how everything blends with the surroundings out here?"

"I've noticed. We went to a furniture store today and there was a bread card in the window. We almost passed it by."

"I know," she said. "The gas station on the corner blends in so well, I feel guilty if I pull in after dinner when he's cutting the grass. It was the council who decided they didn't want commercial businesses to look like commercial businesses. We had enough of that in the city. They wanted them to have that residential feeling."

"That makes a lot of sense," I said.

"I suppose so," she said, "but the other night it was embarrassing. My husband and I went out to dinner and there was a huge line so Russell (my husband) slipped the maître d' $2 and said, 'I think if you'll check your reservations, you'll find we're next. You came personally recommended.'

" 'By whom?' asked the man in the black suit. 'This is a funeral home.' "

As we continued the search for our new home, I

expressed some concern that every time we left the house we'd have to leave a kid on the front porch for a landmark.

"Things will be different," said my husband, "when the builder puts in the shrubbery."

"How much landscaping comes with the house?" I asked.

He tilted his head and recited from memory, "Let's see, we're down for five maples, eight taxus, six evergreens, two ash, four locust, 109 living rose hedge plants, two flowering mother-in-law tongues, and a grove of fifteen assorted, colorful fruit trees."

"Hey, I think this is it," I said, as he pulled into a driveway. "We are officially home!"

We turned the key in the door. My husband and I raced through the house to the backyard to get a glimpse of the flatbed truck and the lift that would turn our barren patch of mud into a jungle. The yard was empty.

"Where's the shrubbery?" asked my husband.

One of the children called from the house, "Mommy! Daddy! The shrubbery is here!"

"Where?" asked my husband.

"On the dining room table with the mail." We stood around the table. No one spoke as we viewed the envelope holding five maples, eight taxus, six evergreens, two ash, four locust, 109 living rose

hedge plants, two flowering mother-in-law tongues, and a grove of fifteen assorted, colorful fruit trees.

My son had more foliage than that growing under his bed.

"Gather it up," said my husband, "and put it in the garage and for God's sake watch the dog. He has eight assorted fruit trees stuck in his tail."

By noon the next day we had planted the entire package.

"Whatya think?" asked my husband.

"It looks like a missile site," I grumbled.

"I think everything will survive the transplanting with the exception of the maple tree. The dog . . ."

"He didn't."

"Yep. His tail brushed against it and the trunk snapped in half."

"I'm worried about the flowering mother-in-law's tongues."

Why?"

"They just spoke to me. They said, 'Help.' "

The Original Settlers

The triumph of man over the suburbs was made possible by the sheer guts of a band of original settlers.

Later, other fringe businesses would sprout up:

a water supply, hospitals, grocery stores, post offices and schools; scouting programs and Good Humor trucks, but at the beginning, these scouts welcomed the newcomers from the city with hands out-stretched—and palms upward.

The Telephone Representative

"Do you want a phone?" asked the lady at the door.

"What kind of a joke is that?" I asked irritably. "Does John Wayne salute the flag? Does Dean Martin drink? Does the Pope work Sundays? Of course I want a phone," I said, literally dragging her into the living room. "Where do I sign?"

"My goodness," she smiled. "Not so fast. We have some decisions to make. First, let me introduce myself. I am Miss Turtletaub, your telephone representative, and I'll be handling your application. Now, to begin with, what type of service do you want?"

"The one where the phone is in the house."

"You're teasing," she said. "Do you want the party line that is quaint, but a drag, the two-party line where you share your phone with an informer, or the popular private service?"

"Private. Now when . . ."

"I assume you want more than one phone in a house of this size. Where is your family room?"

"Down the hall, first door to the left and lock it or the kids will bust in on you."

"Oh. Then what about a phone in your bedroom? After all, there is nothing more frightening than the insistent ring of the phone after midnight when your loved ones need you the most and you are busy breaking your leg in a dark hallway."

"The bedroom sounds great. Could you . . ."

"Three phones. That's smart. Now, what about a jack? After all, basking out of doors is the reason you moved to this cornfield in the first place. Just say you are standing out in the backyard talking to your neighbors. Without a phone nearby, you'll never know when some disc jockey is trying to give away $10,000. Look at it this way—a jackpot like that would pay for the jack in one phone call's time."

"Terrific. One jack. Now could we talk about . . ."

"Color? I knew you were discerning the moment I walked in. I brought along some color chips and I think you'll find coordinated phones for every room in your house. There's God's green, barnyard brown, brothel red, and of course boring black."

"One barnyard, one God's, and one boring."

"Wise choice. Now, have you thought about which model you prefer? We have a great one that hangs from the wall for the kitchen that doesn't take up valuable counter space. Then we have the cradle type with the traditional dial, and we have the collector's gallery: the conversation-piece types in the French provincial, the Early American ones shaped like a pump, and here's a cutesie shaped like an ear trumpet."

"Ah . . . traditional is fine," I said, fidgeting, "now, would you be able to tell me . . ."

"You have to live with it. Now about the listing. I know you have youngsters in the family and most of our sophisticated clientele such as yourself want their children listed so they might reap the entire benefits of a phone."

"That's fine," I said.

"Now, unless you have any questions, I think that does it," she said, smiling and snapping her book shut.

"Just one," I said excitedly. "When can you install the phones?"

She shuffled through her papers and came out with a schedule. Then, tracing down with her fingernail, she paused and said, "A year and a half."

"*A year and a half!*"

"You sound shocked," she smiled. "Have you any

35

idea how much money is involved in cables and poles and electronics to bring phone service all the way out to Suburbian Gems? Why it takes an Act of Congress just to clear the land. We can't perform miracles, can we? Excuse me," she said, "I must dash. There's a couple moving in today down the street. What would they think if the phone company wasn't there to offer their services?'"

The Insurance Salesman

Biff Rah said, "You look familiar. Didn't we go to school together?"

It was a funny thing for a man to say over the telephone.

But that's the way neighborhood insurance men in the suburbs were. They clutched at any straw to establish some common basis for your trust and your signature on an endowment. "Listen," he said, "I know you are busy getting settled. Don't I know it? I'm ten years—and I'm still unpacking, right?"

"The children are a little . . ."

"Hey, kids. Do I know kids?" he said. "Got five of them myself so I understand your problem. All I want to do is to come over and review what you've got in the way of protection, and leave, okay?"

We agreed.

Biff grabbed my hand at the door, pumped it and said, "You look familiar. Didn't we go to school together?"

"Not unless you wore a plaid jumper and knee socks. It was an all-girls' school."

"I was the one with the knobby knees who never shaved!" he grinned, punching me in the arm and knocking me into the bookcases. "But seriously folks," he said, whipping open his briefcase. "I didn't come here to make jokes. I simply dropped by to spell out a few facts of life. You've just moved into a new house, your kids are in their jammies watching TV, you're employed (nodding to my husband), you've got a car, and you (nodding at me) stay home and bake bread. You gotta be like this family here in the picture, right?"

We looked down to a page in his notebook at a picture depicting what had to be the All-American family with straight teeth, healthy gums, yellow hair, tennis sweaters, and a house behind them that looked like the Williamsburg.

"Now, what if this happened?" he asked dramatically and with a small brush that took no longer than fifteen seconds removed my husband from the picture.

"How did you do that?" I asked.

"You're missing the point," he said irritably. "Now what happens to that happy family if Daddy is gone. They're repossessing the car. They're taking the house away. They're taking the furniture away. The children are crying. Mommy doesn't know which way to turn. Now, do you know what that means?"

"It means I get custody of the kids," I snapped.

"It means Daddy didn't make plans."

"It wouldn't be the first time," I snapped.

"Lucky," interrupted Biff, "it's not too late. There is still time to protect your loved ones with this twenty-year-pay life. While you are young, the premiums aren't too bad, but in a few years when you develop those heart problems, circulatory disorders, high blood pressure, and an aneurysm, it may not be available to you at any price."

My husband signed the agreement in mid-air. As I squeezed his hand in appreciation, Biff leaned down and addressed himself to our children. "I can tell by looking at you that Mommy has done a wonderful job. And you're not to blame her when she leaves and you are left alone to shift for yourselves."

"Where am I going?" I asked.

"Face it. It's inevitable that someday you'll be going to that big utility room in the sky. May I ask

you something? How much insurance do you carry on yourself?"

"I don't know," I stammered, "my husband takes care of that."

"I don't like to make trouble," he said, "but usually a man will cover his wife with a policy which he considers to be her value to him."

"How much am I covered for?" I asked.

"You have the basic $96-no-frill-no-fault-burial-policy," he mumbled.

"*Ninety-six bucks!* That wouldn't bury a bird in a shoebox!"

"That's right," said Biff. "Basically what this means is that when you go, they prop you up in a Christian Science reading room, play a record of Perry Como singing 'Don't Fence Me In,' put you on a public bus, and God knows what happens to you."

We signed another policy.

As Biff got up to go he said, "You're such bright people I'm almost embarrassed to ask, but I have a responsibility to you. You are putting aside $50 a week for each child's education aren't you? Don't bother to answer. Of course you are."

"As a matter of fact," said my husband, "we aren't."

Biff shrugged, "Forget I mentioned it. I mean the chances are they'll never need it. Depressed and disappointed at the lack of opportunity, they will drop out of high school, pick up with another drop-out who pumps gas, marry, and live in one room until the baby comes . . ."

"*Stop!*" I shouted. "Tell us what to do."

"Well, there are endowments. They're expensive, but it all depends on what your children are worth to you."

"They're worth everything we own."

"That'll about cover it," he smiled. "Well, you are wonderful people and a great little family and if, by some act of God, the house should burn to the ground, don't fail to call me and I'll try to work something out—contributions from neighbors, a phone call to an agency . . ."

"You mean we're not covered?"

"It's so simple to be covered, it's hardly worth mentioning, but if you'll sign here, it's done." My husband scribbled his signature.

"Listen," said Biff, "I've overstayed my visit. I must be running along. And don't worry about the coverage on your car. Parents are great for pitching in when bad luck strikes. According to statistics, two out of every three cars will be involved in an accident this year, but who knows, you could be

the lucky one. Anyway, welcome to Surburbian Gems—and don't you feel better now?"

The Antique Dealer

Some say the antique syndrome surfaced to offset the newness of the land, the homes, and the settlers.

Some say the interest was initiated by a desire to return to the roots of yesterday.

I contend the entire movement to acquire antiques was born out of sheer respect of things that lasted longer than fifteen minutes.

Whatever the reason, in Suburbian Gems, there was an Eagle over every sofa, a slop jar of geraniums in every bathroom, and a deacon's bench in every hallway.

The weekends found every husband in the neighborhood sanding, sawing, staining, restoring, or stalking every antique dealer and show in the area.

My husband became an antique nut. I never saw a man become so possessed. He brought home white SuppHose, reputedly worn by Thomas Jefferson, a moose's head that had personally witnessed the Battle of Appomattox, and a primitive machine for storing water during the cattle drives west. (I didn't have the heart to tell him he bought the water cooler

in the church hallway where they were holding the sale.)

It's hard to single out any one antique dealer for this documentary. They all had a different "style." Some were "story tellers." My husband loved the "story tellers." They were the ones who if you bought a button would relate how this button was from the uniform of a Confederate soldier who had scratched the name JAY on the back. His brother, who had been visiting north, joined the Union forces and he too had their family name, Jay, scratched on the back of one of his buttons. The two buttons would bring a price of $150. Unfortunately, he had only one, but if we would leave our phone number, when he came across the other one, he would give a call. In less than a week (isn't that unbelievable!) he called to say the other button had been found and was available.

There were the scavenger dealers who were like ambulance chasers. They watched the death notices and anyone over the age of forty-three got a visit from them to appraise and buy goodies from the estate. Scavenger dealers knew only one phrase, "Do you have any idea what we could have gotten for this pitcher/glass/bowl/tumbler/plate/mirror/ etc., had it not been cracked?" My husband loved

the "scavenger dealers." He always felt he was getting a real buy under the table from them.

There were also the "hustlers in bib overalls." These were the little farmers who feigned surprise that someone would want to buy boards from a barn that was ready to fall down.

My husband loved the "barnyard hustlers." He would stop the car, introduce himself, chew on a piece of hay, and talk about how the rains or drought had affected the crops. Then he would venture, "Hey, how much would you want for a couple of those old two-by-fours over there on your barn?"

The farmers would give a little crooked smile and say, "You kiddin' me, mister? You mean those old faded, weathered boards, wormy with termites on that barn that a good wind would knock over?"

"Those are the ones," said my husband.

"Oh, I suppose $50 would put 'em in your trunk."

We were dealing with pros.

If I had to name one original settler who was known by everyone, it would have to be Miss Emma. Miss Emma was a sweet, little old lady whose farmhouse in the suburbs stuck out like a birth-control clinic in a retirement community.

There was no quaint sign flapping from her lamppost proclaiming, "ANTIQUES." She never ad-

vertised. Never brought her wares to a show at the church. The word just got around that if Miss Emma answered the door on that particular day and was in a good mood, she "might" sell you some of her precious heirlooms right out from under her.

In truth, Miss Emma should have been voted by the Academy of Arts and Sciences as the year's Best Actress of any year.

Responding to your knock, she would open the door a crack and say, "Today isn't a good day. Come back—say tomorrow?" which only made you more determined to somehow smuggle a checkbook into that house and cart away half of its furnishings.

Once inside, if you expressed an interest in, say a desk, she would throw her body in front of it protectively and say, "Oh no, this is the one thing I couldn't possibly sell. Martin (her late husband) would come right out of his grave. You see, it belonged to his great-grandmother who got it from a General Washburn."

"Are you sure it was Washburn? Could it have been Washington?"

"Could be. Great-grandma Tucker was a little hard of hearing."

Five minutes later, the desk would be in the back of someone's trunk and on its way to a place of prominence to be treated as a member of the family.

My husband and I begged her to let us come in

one Saturday. "Only if you don't stay too long," she agreed. Then my husband spotted it. One of the most enormous wooden bowls we had ever seen. "How much would you sell this bowl for, Miss Emma?" asked my husband.

She jumped between the bowl and my husband. "This bowl is not for sale. You may buy anything in this house, but not this bowl."

At that moment I knew that if I didn't have that bowl, I would not continue breathing. "Please, Miss Emma, we'd give it a good home and cherish it as you have cherished it."

"It's been in our family for generations," she said sadly. "I can remember my grandmother bathing the babies in it (my throat hurt and I wanted to cry). My mother used to bake bread in it—ten loaves at a time—and I just keep it around to store apples in it for the little children who visit."

"I know," I sobbed, "I know and I will do likewise."

A few minutes and a substantial check later, we were headed home with the bowl. "Do you know what I'm going to do with that bowl?" asked my husband. "I'm going to sand it down and then varnish it with a clear varnish and keep it in a natural state. We can put it on our divider and keep bright, shiny apples in it all the time."

He must have put in 184 man hours on that bowl. Every night in the garage I heard him sanding away. Then one night he came into the bedroom from the garage and said, "I don't believe it. I sanded all the way down through the stain and do you know what I found? (I shook my head.) MADE IN JAPAN. That can only mean one thing."

"What?" I asked excitedly.

"That Great-grandmother Tucker was Japanese. We've got an oriental antique on our hands."

We were elated, of course, and spared no time in telling our antique enthusiasts about our "find."

"Is it a huge wooden bowl with a crack down the middle?" asked the Martins.

"Yes! You've heard of it!"

"Heard of it? We got one too," said the Martins. "So have the Palmers and the Judsons."

"You're kidding! Where did they get theirs?"

"Miss Emma's."

During the next few years Miss Emma's family heirlooms became as standard in Surburbian Gems as doorknobs.

It's funny. In the five or six years everyone bought furniture out of Miss Emma's house, the house always was filled and always looked the same. You'd have thought someone would have noticed.

CHAPTER TWO

Major Battles Fought
in the Suburbs

Finding the Builder Who Built the House (1945-1954)

Edward C. Phlegg, the builder of Suburban Gems, made Howard Hughes look like an exhibitionist.

No one had ever seen him. His phone number was a candy store that took messages. The billboards bearing his picture showed only the back of his head.

"If it's an emergency," said my husband, "I suppose I could track him down."

"Well, every time I push down the toaster, the garage door goes up. The hot-water heater is

hooked up to the garden hose and I am sautéeing the lawn. The sliding-glass doors don't slide. The wall heats up when I turn on the porch light. The hall toilet does not accept tissue. Half of our driveway is on our neighbor's property, the grapes on the kitchen wallpaper are growing upside down, and I have a sign on our front door reading, 'OUT OF ORDER! PLEASE USE HOUSE NEXT DOOR.' "

"I think our best bet is to try and pin down the contractors," said my husband. "I'll see what I can do."

Two months later, we had tracked down our plumber. He had defected to a small country behind the iron curtain taking with him the last of the 1/15-inch pipe used in our bathrooms. Delivery was guaranteed in three years.

Our electrician was facing charges of involuntary arson of a large office building where political corruption was suspect. (He contended his bid was the lowest offered—a case of Coors.)

Our building foreman had returned to high school. He explained it had only been a temporary summer job to earn enough for a bicycle.

Our furnace man was living under an assumed name in Yuma, Arizona.

Our painter was drying out in a Sanitorium in upper New York State.

And our concrete man was studying contract law at the University of Cincinnati.

"I don't want to panic you," said my husband, "but I think we're stuck with our own repairs."

"Why should I panic? Just because when our water pipes sweat you prescribed an anti-perspirant?"

"Oh c'mon."

"Just because you were too embarrassed to ask for a male or a female plug at the hardware store and I had to write you a note."

"You made your point."

"Just because we have the only toilet in the block reseated with Play Doh . . ."

"Look," he said, "did you marry for love or did you marry to have your toilet fixed?"

When I didn't answer he said, "I'll get my toolbox and we can talk about what has to be done."

He set down a small fishing tackle box that had been originally inscribed "FIRST AID." This had been crossed out and "TOLS" was misspelled across the top in pencil.

Inside was a cork, five feet of pink, plastic clothesline, a small hammer, a flashlight with no batteries, a curler, a poker chip, and a book of rain-soaked matches.

"This is it?"

"This is it. What do you need first?" he asked.

"Storm windows for the entire house."

"Are you crazy?" he gasped. "I'll need a miter box."

"I thought we sprayed for them."

"Couldn't I start with something easy—like a revolving door?"

"As a matter of fact, you could make one of those little doors for the dog that saves you from letting them in and out all the time. You know, the one with the little hinges that flap in and out?"

"Right," he said. "No problem. You just saw a little hole in the door, attach the hinges and you're in business."

When I left him he was standing the dog against the wall with a tape measure and saying, "Let's see how much you've grown today."

A few hours later I felt a draft in the bedrooms and went to check. You could have slung a herd of buffalo through the little hole in the door.

"Don't worry," he cautioned, "the door on it will eliminate the wind whistling through."

"Now what are you doing?" I asked, as he dropped to his hands and knees.

"Showing the dog how to go through it. Dogs have to be taught, you know. But they're great little

mimics." He twisted and groaned until his body was halfway through the door.

"What's wrong?" I asked.

"I'm stuck."

"Which end do you want me to save?"

"Will you knock it off with the jokes? Here I am with half of my body on the front porch and the other half in the hallway and . . ."

"Would you be terribly upset if I opened the door right now?"

"Why?"

"The dog has to go out."

"Well, hurry up. When I'm finished here, I want to start on the storm windows."

The search for Edward C. Phlegg continued for nine years. Someone thought they spotted the back of his head at an Arthur Fiedler concert. Another neighbor heard he was involved in selling beachfront property in Fargo, North Dakota.

Whatever, we never saw the builder of Suburbian Gems face to face.

Then one day we opened our newspaper and saw where Edward C. Phlegg had died. His funeral was one of the biggest the city had ever known. Mourners from Suburbian Gems alone filled the church. (Contractors who hadn't been paid couldn't even get inside.)

There wasn't a dry eye in the church.

We were saying good-bye to the only man who knew where in Hong Kong our furnace was made. Who alone knew the secret ingredients of our patios that bubbled when the sun hit them. Who would take with him his reasons for slanting the roof toward the center of the house and burying the septic tank under the living room floor.

As we stood in the cemetery mourning our loss, there was a flash of lightning and a rumble of thunder as before our very eyes, the large stone bearing the name Edward C. Phlegg sunk to one side and remained at a 40-degree angle.

There was no doubt in our minds. God was trying to tell us that Mr. Phlegg had gone to that big Escrow in the sky.

The Second-Car Ten-Day War

We had talked about the isolation of the suburbs and the expense of a second car before moving there and I thought I had made my position very clear.

I did not want a car. Did not need a car. And would not take a car if it were offered me.

I lied.

"I've got to have wheels," I said to my husband one night after dinner.

"We've talked about this before," he said, "and we agreed that the reason we migrated was to explore all the adventures the suburbs has to offer."

"I've explored both of them. Now I need a car. A car will put me in touch with the outside world. It will be my link with another culture, another civilization, another world of trade."

"Aren't you being a little dramatic?" he suggested.

"Let me lay it on you, Cleavie, the high spot in my day is taking knots out of shoestrings—with my teeth—that a kid has wet on all day long. I'm beginning to have feelings for my shower-massage pik. Yesterday, I etched a dirty word on the leaf of my philodendron."

"And you think a car is going to help you?"

"Of course it will help. I'll be able to go to the store, join a bowling league, have lunch downtown with the girls, volunteer, go to the dentist, take long drives in the country. I want to see the big, outside world from atop a lube rack. I want to whirl dizzily in a cloud of exhaust, rotate my tires with the rest of the girls. Don't you understand? I want to *honk* if I love Jesus!"

For a reason I was soon to understand, *all* of us

went to the showroom to pick out *my* car. Within minutes, I saw it. It was a bright yellow sports number—a one-seater that puts you three inches off the ground and sounds like a volcano when the motor turns over. Near to ecstasy, I closed my eyes and imagined myself at a traffic light, my large sunglasses on top of my head like Marlo Thomas, and as I quickly brushed lip gloss on my lips from a small pot, a dark stranger from the car next to me shouted, "Could we meet and talk?" And I laughed cruelly, "Don't be a fool! I'm a homeroom mother!" and sped off.

The rest of the family was gathered around a four-wheel-drive station wagon with a spare tire on top, space for extra gas cans along the back and fold-down seats giving you room to transport the Cleveland Symphony and all their instruments.

"Hey, is this a car?" asked my husband, his eyes shining.

"That was *my* next question," I said. "Look, I don't want transportation to a war, I just want a car to take me to the store and back."

"Of course you do," he said, "and this is the no-nonsense car that can get the job done."

Oh, I tried all right to hide my disappointment. I put glasses on top of my head, touched up my lip gloss at traffic lights, and even occasionally ran my

tongue over my lips like Jennifer O'Neill, but I never climbed behind the wheel of that orthopedic vehicle without feeling like I was following General Patton into Belgium.

Besides, I was the only woman in the neighborhood with a big wagon. All the others tooled around in small, sleek, sports cars that had previously belonged to their husbands.

By the end of the first week, the newness of owning my own car had begun to wear off. I had transported six kids a day to school, a power mower to the repair shop, a porch swing for a garage sale, and the neighbor's dog to the vet who would not fit into a Volkswagen, Nova, Pontiac, Plymouth, Oldsmobile, Tank, or Global Van Lines.

The second week things picked up. I transported thirty-five sleeping bags and supplies for a week at camp, paneling from a lumber yard which wouldn't make delivery until the following week, a missile launch for a science fair, eight baseball bats, four base bags and twelve Little-League players, eight bags of fertilizer for the lawn and six surly homeroom mothers who arrived at a tea smelling like fertilizer.

It was of no comfort to me whatsoever knowing that I would make U-Haul Mother of the Year. I had to unload that car. Things came to a head one

afternoon when I stopped for a traffic light and a huge transport truck pulled alongside me. The ones that travel all night to get your bread fresh to you in the morning. While waiting for the light to change, a burly driver looked over and shouted, "Hey, Mac, where's a good place to eat and get some sack time?"

I knew then I had to make my move and trade up—to my husband's car.

"You don't suppose we could switch cars?" I asked that night after dinner.

"Why would we want to do a thing like that?" he asked.

I hesitated dramatically, "I didn't want to tell you but the children get drowsy in the back seat. I think something is leaking in."

"Then, by all means, take it to the garage and have it fixed." (STRIKE ONE.)

"I'm in the garage so often now, I have my own key to the restroom. What would you say if I told you I only get seven miles to the gallon and I'm costing you $1.50 every time I wait for a light to turn green?"

"We knew the car would be an added expense when we bought it." (STRIKE TWO.)

"It's really a shame for your new, small, compact, car to sit out all day in the harsh sun and the rain

and the cold when it could sit in a nice, warm garage."

"There's something to that, but how would you transport all those children every day?" (BALL ONE.)

"I just read a survey that a smaller car is safer because the children are packed together and do not have room to swing around and argue about who gets a window."

"That makes sense (BALL TWO) but what would I do with a big car that eats gas and attracts burly truck drivers?" (BALL THREE.)

It was three and two and I wound up for the big one.

"In a way it's a shame you don't have the station wagon. That way you could pick up some paying riders who would love transportation to the city. The extra money would pay for your gas."

HOME RUN!

"It's funny you should mention that," he said. "The Osborn's daughter, Fluffy, asked me just the other day if I had room in my car for her to ride to the city."

"You mean the girl in the next block who always looks like she's wearing a life preserver?"

"What a thing to say. She just has good posture."

"That's inflatable—I mean debatable."

"Then it's settled. We trade cars. You can drive mine and I'll take the wagon."

I never knew victory could make you feel so rotten.

Getting Sex Out of the Schools and Back into the Gutter Where It Belongs

My son was five years old when his teacher sent home a note informing me he was sexually immature.

I confronted her the next day after school and said, "What is this supposed to mean, Mrs. Kravitz?"

"It means we had a little quiz the other day on reproductive organs and he defined every one of them as an Askyourfather. You are sending a child into the world, Mrs. Bombeck, who thinks Masters and Johnson is a golf tournament and fertilization is something you do in the fall to make the lawns green."

"That's true," I nodded.

"Have you ever discussed sex in your home?" she asked.

"No, but once he caught Barbie and Ken together in a cardboard car in their underwear."

"Have you ever discussed with him the parts of his body?"

"Only those that showed dirt."

"You have to do better than that. This is a new day, Mrs. Bombeck. We don't hide our heads in the sand any more. Suburban schools are taking the lead in informing our young people about sex at an early age. For example, I am expecting a baby and I told the class about it."

"You told them you had something in the oven?" I asked incredulously.

"I told them I was pregnant!" she said.

I bit my finger. "Good Lord, Mrs. Kravitz. I didn't know why my husband gasped every time Lassie cleared the fence until I was twenty-six."

"Then you had better get used to it," she said. "Your son is about to be informed."

The suburbs didn't invent sex—it only gave it a wider distribution. No one could have known the ramifications sex education could have had in the community. Little boys wrote dirty sayings on the sidewalks with chalk as they always did, but adults didn't protest. They didn't understand what they meant.

Parents who tried to deal directly with their children by saying, "Look, Brucie, there seems to be some confusion between sexual and asexual reproduction," were only to be interrupted with, "Look, Dad, you should have come to me sooner. What do you need to know?"

Eavesdropping (among young people) dropped off 75 percent but increased 86 percent among adults. And one second grader confronted his parents one night with, "You little devils, you. And you told me I was conceived without sin."

Things had clearly gotten out of hand and we knew it. So, a meeting was called at the school to discuss the future of sex education.

"Frankly," said the librarian, "I'm worried. Do you realize the new *National Geographic* has been in for three weeks and has not been checked out once by a third grader?"

We gasped. "The youngsters don't want to play Doctor and Nursie any more," said a distraught father. "My son wants to open up his own office."

"I'm afraid," said Ken Kinsey, "that the impact of sex education goes even deeper. We now have before us the problem of dress code. It seems with the laxity of certain rules and the casualness with which we are regarding the human body, some youngsters are coming to school in various attire.

Tonight, we have been asked to consider the outcome of displaying—(he swallowed hard)—the navel."

The librarian sucked in her breath. The co-chairman cleared his throat and I grabbed for my son's sex manual to see if it had a double meaning.

"It seems," continued Ken, "that many of our little girls have been wearing jeans that fit around the hips and shirts that hang just below the rib cage and there is a bare area in between that needs some clarification. Anyone have any ideas?"

"Well, I have always felt if the Good Lord had meant for people to go nude He would never have invented the wicker chair," said one mother.

"That is a good point," said Ken. "Anyone else?"

"Have we established what a navel is?" asked a teacher.

"I think it is safe to assume that most of us are familiar with the navel . . ."

"Wait a minute," said a mother, "there are navels and there are navels. I mean some are 'outies' and some are 'innies.' I personally find the outies disgusting."

"That's strange," said her husband, "I find them sexy."

"You don't know how strange," said his wife. "I

have an 'innie' and demand to know where you've seen an 'outie.' "

"Please people. Let's get back to the issue here. Should we permit the navel to be displayed in a classroom atmosphere?"

"Today the navel, tomorrow the buttock," grumbled the math teacher.

"It seems to me," said a parent, "that if lax dress codes are allowed to continue, we may be in for something that only the National Guard can handle."

"I worry," said a mother who had been sitting quietly, "that it will blow the lid off a whole can of emotions. I mean, how do you expect a six-year-old to stay in the lines when he colors if he is distracted by a bared navel sitting at the desk next to his."

"That's a good point, Ethel," said Ken.

"I see nothing wrong with navels," said a militant in the rear. "Why are all of you so hung up over something as normal as a navel?"

"Navels are not on trial here," interrupted Ken. "It's simply we must draw the line somewhere with the relaxing of morals among our young people."

"So, if you're ashamed of your navel," persisted the militant, "I'll put a Band-Aid over it."

"What does the U.S. government say about navels?" asked a businessman.

"To my knowledge, there is no department at the moment that is conducting any sort of findings on the subject," said Ken. "If we could just get back to the subject . . ."

"If you ask me," said a concerned mother, "I think by our condoning navels in a public-school building, we are lowering the age of puberty. Next thing you know, we will permit them to have acne before they are ten and lower their voices at nine. I say they are growing up too fast. Let's save the navels for later when they can handle them and enjoy them like adults."

There was a round of applause and a few in the back stood up and said, "Here, here."

"Should we put it to a vote?" asked Ken. "Okay, all of you in favor of issuing a dress code in which navels must be covered, signify by saying, 'Aye' (a roar). Opposed? (One, 'You bet your sweet umbilical cord!')

"Now, the next thing on the agenda," said Ken nervously, "is Miss Barker, who teaches the third-graders human sexuality, would like to have a lab . . ."

I slipped out the back door. I wanted time to consider the ramifications, the objectives, the impact

of bringing such a program within my child's learning processes. Also, to have my six-year-old explain to me what human sexuality is.

Saving the Recession from a Depression

Following World War II, when the nation began its migration to the suburbs, there was fear that the economy would give way to a period of depression.

There entered upon the scene three commodities destined to bring the country to its economic feet again: The Picture Window, the Green-Lawn Syndrome, and two teenage dolls, Barbie and Ken.

No one could have imagined the impact these three items had on the spending habits of the settlers. In retrospect, it was simply a matter of figuring the odds. Thirty-million suburbanites, all supporting and maintaining a picture window, green grass, and two naked dolls—it would have brought any nation out of the darkness of despair and into prosperity once more.

The Picture Window

To build a house in the suburbs without at least one picture window was considered un-American.

I personally knew my heart would stop beating if I did not have one.

As I said to my husband, "Imagine! A window with nine feet of glass that would invite the sunshine in during the day and reflect the stars at night. That would reveal neighbors waving a friendly 'hello.' That would allow the gentle breezes of a summer night to come indoors and hold the snow of winter at bay with its frosty patterns on the glass. Who would need any form of entertainment with nature's panorama changing with the seasons. Who would need rewards in this life other than viewing happy children at play?"

"You got the picture window," he said helplessly.

Two days later, I said, "The man is coming today to cover the picture window. It will cost $500."

"Cover the window!" he gasped. "What about your 'inviting the sunshine in during the day and reflecting the stars at night?'"

"That sun is blinding me. I can't get away from it. And the dog is beginning to tan. As for stars, forget it. The only thing that window attracts at night are window peepers."

A month later I informed my husband, "The furniture has to be covered. It will cost $800."

"But it's always been good enough for us."

"Exactly, but is it good enough for the 'neighbors

waving a friendly hello' through our picture window?"

"But I thought we got the windows covered."

"You can't keep the curtains drawn on a picture window all of the time or people will think you have something to hide."

Four months to the day, I casually mentioned the picture window would need storm covering and screen. They would run about $400.

"Wait a minute," he charged, "is this the same woman who said she 'was going to allow the gentle breezes of a summer night to come indoors and hold the snow of winter at bay with its frosty patterns on the glass'?"

"That's before I realized the summer breezes harbor mosquitoes that suck your blood. Besides, I've had it with those 'frosty patterns on the glass.' The window is causing frosty patterns on the children's lungs and our walls look like a waterfall."

We were two weeks into summer when I informed my husband, "We are getting a liner to block out the light of our window so we can watch TV during the daytime. It will cost $150."

His head jerked up sharply, "What happened to 'nature's panorama changing with the seasons before your eyes'?"

"Nature's panorama has deteriorated into a view

of old Mr. Hudson framed in his picture window in his underwear scratching his stomach and picking his teeth with a matchbook cover."

One night I met my husband at the door. "We are getting Picture Window insurance. It will cost $28 a year."

"I don't believe this," he said. "When did you become disenchanted with the 'rewards of viewing happy children at play'?"

"When Michael Ormstead's baseball came crashing through our picture window. Meanwhile, we will have to have this one replaced. It will cost $160."

I had never seen my husband bite his necktie in half before.

The Suburban Lawn

Never, in the history of the world, have so many men sacrificed so much, so often, at such a price, for so little.

The green grass is what lured settlers to the wilderness in the first place. They wanted to cultivate a little patch of greenery that would tickle the feet of their barefooted babies, cushion their falls, and cradle them in the bosom of the soil.

It seemed incongruous in the quiet of an evening to hear a father pull his son close to him and say, "*You cut across that lawn one more time, Gilbert, and I'm going to break every bone in your body.*"

The suburban lawn not only became an obsession with the suburban husband, it became the very symbol of manhood. Not to have a lawn was like admitting you turned off the Super Bowl to take a nap, used deodorant shields in your T-shirts, or had training wheels on your Harley-Davidson. Every casual greeting opened with: "How's the lawn, Buddy?" "Hey, Frank, see you got your crabgrass on the run." Or "Set your blade down an inch, Buck. We all did."

Keeping up with a couple of hundred lawn enthusiasts was not only back-breaking, it was downright expensive. No one knew it any better than one poor devil in Suburban Gems who divorced his wife. His name was Lyle Link. The settlement was rumored to be the stiffest decision ever handed down in a court of law.

Lyle's wife received no alimony, no support whatsoever for the children, and she assumed payments on the house, the car, and the furniture.

Lyle got custody of the lawn.

It was like being on parole. He couldn't leave

the state. He couldn't afford to remarry and there wasn't time to drink.

There were fertilizers, weed killers, maintenance, and keeping up with his neighbors. Lyle was spending more time at home than he ever did when he was married.

There wasn't a night he was not hauling bags of manure and nitrogen, trimming around walks and trees on his hands and knees, watering, mulching, and clipping.

Lyle started out with a hand mower, but eventually bowed to neighborhood pressure and got a rotary mower. This led to a lawn sweeper to pick up the grass, and an electric lawn trimmer to get close to the walk, and a spreader to evenly distribute new seed and fertilizer.

Every week there was some new gimmick to buy that sent everyone racing to the garden center. One evening as Lyle was tooling around in his riding mower with the reclining bucket seats and the console dashboard—his automatic sprinkler creeping along silently over the green carpet, his hedges topped perfectly with his electric hedge clipper, his trees being fed automatically just the right amounts of iron and nitrogen—his neighbor dropped by and said, "Too bad about your lawn, Lyle."

Lyle shut off his motor and paled slightly. "What do you mean, 'Too bad about my lawn'?"

"The whole neighborhood is talking about it. I thought you knew."

"Knew what? For God's sake tell me."

"Your lawn has root rot nematode."

Lyle's eyes misted. "Are you sure?"

"Didn't you see the little brown spots that never seemed to get better when you watered them?"

"And it's such a young lawn," said Lyle. "How long does it have?"

"With no bicycles, sleds, or kids running over it, I give it about a year."

"Well, we're not going to give up," said Lyle, squaring his shoulders, "they come up with new things every day. We're going to fight!" he said, heading out toward the garden center.

"Hey," yelled his neighbor, "maybe this isn't the time to bring it up, but I heard your wife is getting remarried."

Lyle turned slowly, disgust written plainly on his face. "What kind of an animal are you?" he asked, his voice quavering with emotion. "First you come here and tell me my lawn has root rot nematode and there's nothing anyone can do to save it and at best it only has a year to live, and then you babble on about my wife remarrying.

Who cares? Don't you understand? If my lawn dies, I don't want to go on living any more. Leave me alone."

As his neighbor retreated, Lyle got down on his hands and knees and sobbed, "We'll travel. That's what we'll do—just you and me. We'll visit the White House lawn, the grounds at Mt. Vernon, maybe upper New York State where the grass is green most of the time and you can make new friends . . ."

Barbie and Ken

The real lifesaver of the economy was a pair of teenage dolls who appeared ironically one Christmas stacked (excuse the expression) among the baby dolls who burped, ate, cried, wet, walked, and were as sexless as a stick of gum.

My daughter picked Barbie up off the counter and exclaimed, "Look, Mommy, here is a doll that looks just like you."

I checked out the two-and-a-half-inch bust, the three-inch hips, and the legs that looked like two filter tips without tobacco and said, "She looks like she just whipped through puberty in fifteen minutes."

"I want her," my daughter whined.

Barbie cost $5.98 in the buff, so we purchased a little dress, a pair of pumps, a bra, and a pair of briefs that came to $6.95.

"Aren't we going to buy her a girdle?" asked my daughter.

"Let's wait until she eats and see if she needs one," I said.

If any of us believed for a moment that Barbie was going to be happy as a simple housewife, we were in for a surprise. Barbie was a swinger and she needed the wardrobe to do it.

Within a week, she had three lounge outfits ($5.95 each), an entire pool ensemble ($4.95), two formals ($7.95 each), a traveling suit ($6.95), and skating outfit ($5.00).

One afternoon as I was on my hands and knees fishing Barbie's beach ball out of the sweeper bag, my daughter announced, "Barbie's lonely."

"Terrific!" I said. "Why don't you mail her to Camp Pendleton. And send her satin sheets with her."

"I think we ought to buy Ken."

There was something weird about Ken, but I couldn't put my finger on it. He was a taller version of Barbie who came wearing a jock strap and an insincere smile. He cost $5.98. Within a week, his

wardrobe consisted of tennis attire ($7.95), jump suit ($4.95), white tuxedo ($10.95), and a terry cloth robe ($3.95), plus a cardboard car ($12.95). As I explained to my husband, "You don't expect them to sit around night after night passing a beach ball back and forth, do you?"

The little freaks were draining our budget, but I bought some of the patterns and was able to satisfy their clothing appetite by sitting at the sewing machine day and night.

Then one day my daughter announced, "Ken and Barbie are getting married."

It seemed reasonable. After all, they were thrown together day after day in a shoe box under the bed and they were only human.

"What exactly does this mean to me?" I asked.

"Barbie has to have a wedding dress ($10.95) and a trousseau ($36.50) and Ken has to have a tuxedo."

"What's wrong with his white one?" I asked.

"That's for dancing—not marrying," she said.

"Anything else?"

"A wedding party."

"A what!"

"We have to buy Midge and some more people so they'll have people at their wedding."

"Can't you invite some of your other dolls?"

"Would you want someone at your wedding with bowed legs and diapers?"

The wedding was the social event of the year. Our gift to them was a cardboard house that looked like the Hilton.

It was months before all the bills were in but I figured the worst was over. Some families on the block were just starting with their first doll. All that was behind us now.

Then one afternoon in the kitchen, my daughter said excitedly, "Guess what? Barbie's going to have a baby. You're going to be a grandmother."

My eyes welled with self-pity as I ticked off the needs—one naked doctor (who played golf on Wednesdays), two naked nurses (who snorkeled on weekends), one ambulance driver in the buff who skied, an unclothed intern who . . .

CHAPTER THREE

The Great Plastic Rush

"You Will Come to My Home Party"

One day, a typical suburban housewife was storing a leftover in a small, plastic bowl. As she pushed down the center of the lid with her thumb, a whooshing sound came out and her neighbor, who was having coffee, said, "Did you just belch?"

"Of course not," she smiled, "I am burping my Suckerware."

"Burping your Suckerware?"

"Right. I find when you force all the air out of your plastic bowl, your cantaloupe will keep for days in your refrigerator."

This was the beginning of the Great Plastic Rush. Within weeks, news had spread throughout the country and the city and women were coming on buses, cars, and bicycles to witness this religious experience.

They did not go home empty handed. The Home Party was born and there was no stopping its growth.

This is how it worked. A housewife, motivated by the promise of a leftover tote bag, would invite twenty of her dearest friends to a party in her home.

Once inside, a professional pitchman would guide the guests to a dining room table laden with wares, and then oil his way through the group with an order form and a ballpoint pen.

No one was forced to go to a home party.

You went out of pure fellowship, need, and unsolicited fear. Fear that when you were tapped to host a party, no one would show up if you didn't go to theirs.

For an added incentive, you played games like "Dessert Bingo" to see how many words you could make out of the word "Leftover."

The plastics were the first to arrive on the suburban scene, but not for long. They were followed by the discovery of Whatever Cookware,

Sarah Covet-thy-neighbor Jewelry, One-Size-Fits-All Sportswear, Bow-Wow Cosmetics, and many more.

Probably the most boring party I ever attended was hosted by the Whatever Cookware company. The Burley brothers (two manufacturer's representatives) came to our house early to cook the entire dinner in their pots that locked in flavor and held captive all the natural juices.

The natural juices weren't the only thing held captive. As we sat around drinking celery cocktails I turned to my husband and asked, "So, whatya wanta do now?"

"We could check the expiration dates on our driver's licenses."

"I want to go home," I said stubbornly.

"You *are* home," he said. "What time do these birds serve dinner? I don't smell anything cooking."

"Of course you can't smell anything. The food is wallowing in its own juices which are locked in under the flavor-sealed lids."

Finally, one of the Burley brothers announced, "Dinner is served." That was only the beginning of the pitch. The Burleys were everywhere. At our elbows grinning, "Is that the most delicious roast you have ever put into your mouth? You have permission to talk with your mouth full."

"How's it going over here, guy? Here, give me your fork. Do you see how I can press it against this Brussels sprout and the juices continue to flow?"

"Don't get up. What do you need? No salt, guy, please. Learn to eat au naturel. The taste buds will adjust to it in time."

"Do you detect just a hint of mint? Ahh, you are discerning."

"Eat the jackets!" he commanded one guest who was scooping out his potatoes. "Look at this folks. He's leaving all the nutrition on his plate."

Following the dinner, we arranged our chairs into rows and watched a double feature: "The Birth of Grease" and "An Enzyme Visits New York."

One Thursday night as I was preparing to go to a home hair-coloring party, I got a call from Dollie Sullivan.

"Guess what?" she said excitedly. "I am giving a plant party. Can you come?"

"What is a plant party?" I asked.

"It's where you bring your sick plants to be healed and to buy new ones. It's really different," she said and hung up.

I figured, why not?

The plant party attracted a group of people I had never seen before. I had been there only five

minutes when someone wanted to go halvsies on a 100-pound bag of manure and a perfect stranger showed me her aphids.

"Girls! Girls!" said the plant representative, "I hate to break this up, but we've got a lot of ground to cover this evening. No pun intended. First, I want to introduce you to my friends." Gathered around her on little chairs were a ha'f dozen or so potted plants. She began to introduce them one by one. "This is Florence Floribunda, Polly Pothus, Ginny Geranium, Irene Iris, Dorothy Daffodil, and Phyllis Potbound—we'll talk more about Phyllis later.

"Now, before we get to the sickies, I want each of you to answer roll call with your favorite insecticide.

"Very good," she said when we had finished. "Now you all have an opportunity to find out about how to deal with your sick plants, so if you'll bring them up one at a time, we'll talk about them."

The first was a woman who was near tears.

"What seems to be the problem?" asked the leader.

"They have icky boo boo on the leaves," she sobbed.

"You're not being too scientific, but I know what boo boo in the back? In Latin, it's called *primus*

you mean," she smiled. "Can all of you see the icky *blosis*. Its common name is dust. When a leaf is covered with five or six years of dust, it can't breathe. It suffocates."

"What should I do?" asked the woman.

"Let's do something gutsy," she said. "Let's wash it." (The crowd cheered.)

Next up was a woman whose plant was in the final stages of deterioration. The leaves were ashen and crumpled limply to the floor. The leader studied it carefully. "Do you talk to your plant? Give it encouragement? The will to live? The incentive to grow?"

"I talked to it yesterday," she said, "but I didn't talk very nice to it. I called it something."

"What did you call it?" asked the plant lady.

The owner whispered the word in the leader's ear. She too turned ashen and crumpled limply to the floor.

Toward the end of the evening, we were given the opportunity to buy fresh, new plants to refurbish the ones in our homes. I chose a beautiful split-leaf philodendron with shiny, green leaves in a pot of mulch fluffed up at its feet like a pillow. That night as I paced the floor with the plant over my shoulder I patted it gently and thought, "What the heck. It beats burping Suckerware."

CHAPTER FOUR

Hazards of Suburban Living

The Car Pool Crouch

A lot of my neighbors suffered from the Car Pool Crouch. It was one of those dreaded diseases you say can never happen to you.

Then one afternoon when you are attending a tea, someone will point out that your knees are apart and your right foot is extended out in an accelerator position. Your elbows are bent slightly and you are holding your purse in front of you like a steering wheel. When a woman leans forward next to you, your arm automatically goes out to catch her when she hits the windshield that isn't there.

You've got it. The Car Pool Crouch.

I have seen perfectly healthy, young, upright women climb into a car in September. By spring, they walked like Groucho Marx.

Out of this malady came the invention of the drive-in. A lot of people think the drive-in was born out of convenience. That's not true. It was born out of desperation of a community of women who could no longer get in and out of their cars.

I once went for an entire week behind the wheel of the car and never missed a beat running my house.

I drove the children to school, idling my motor as they tumbled out of the back seat.

Then it was on to the bank where I pulled in to within inches of the window, slid my check under a bean bag in the drawer, and massaged my legs as I waited.

With money by my side, I next pulled into the cleaners where I left off a bundle and was rewarded with hangers full of clean ones.

At the film service drive-in, I barely had to slow down the car. Just make a hook shot and promise to be back by tomorrow.

At the service station, I sat numbly while he checked my oil, my water, and cleaned off my glasses.

Then it was lunchtime and into a drive-in eatery for a quick bite.

Positioning my wheels on the pulley, I sat in my car while I went through the car wash, feeling just a little uncomfortable with the numbness that was causing shooting back pains.

But there was the post office that had to be driven through and then it was time to pick up the children.

Naturally, we drove to a drive-in for a slushee treat and as dusk was approaching, we hit for a drive-in movie.

On the seventh day, my husband said, "Look, you've been in that car all week. You're pale. You need fresh air. You are also very short. Let's go to that new church everyone is talking about over on Rural Road."

I dressed carefully. And painfully. It had been a long time.

Hesitating, I climbed into the car. It was a drive-in church.

As I sat listening to the voice of the minister on the speaker, I heard him say, "This is the time to pray for any special favors you might wish from God."

I opened my door and with great effort, pushed my legs out. Steadying myself, I grabbed onto the

car with my hands and pulled myself up to my feet. I was standing.

From the other cars, I heard the applause, the voices raised in awe. Some blew their horns. "It's a miracle . . . a miracle!"

The Neighborhood Nomad

My husband put down his paper at breakfast one morning and said, "How many children do we have?"

"Three," I answered quickly.

"Then how come we have four children at breakfast every morning and at dinner each evening?"

I put down the cereal box and studied each one carefully. There was no mistaking the one boy. He had my husband's eyes and the girl definitely had my coloring. But the other two could have been phoned in.

"There's only one way to settle it," said my husband. "Will the real Bombecks please stand up."

They exchanged sheepish glances, a chair scraped, one started to get up, then sat down and finally, three got to their feet.

We all looked at Kenny who sat there staring at a piece of dry toast.

"Son of a gun," said my husband, "I didn't know Kenny wasn't ours. And I just apologized to him yesterday for not spending more time with him."

"How do you think I feel?" I snarled. "I just got him toilet trained!"

When we pressed for details, it seems a little over a year ago, Kenny had wandered into our house to use the bathroom, liked it, and sorta hung around.

"How did you know where our bathroom was?" I asked.

"You have the Pee Wee model just like ours— only with a fireplace. I like a fireplace."

"Doesn't your mother worry about you?" I asked.

"She knows where I am."

"I think I met her. We both went to your parent-teacher conference. At the time I thought she was being a little pushy when she wanted to see your attendance record."

I went to the phone and dialed Kenny's mother. "Mrs. Wick," I said, "I am bringing Kenny home."

"Who?" she asked.

"Kenny, your son."

"Has he been acting up?" she asked.

"No, I just feel Kenny has been with us too long."

"Why do you say that?"

"Because my husband and I just realized we postponed our vacation because we couldn't get anyone to sit with Kenny."

"I understand," she said.

Kenny was right. Their house plan was identical to ours with the exception of a driveway lamp (extra) and colored bathroom fixtures (also extra).

I couldn't help but feel a twinge of guilt as I watched Mrs. Wick bustle around with her brood. No wonder she hadn't missed Kenny. The house was crawling with children.

"Joey, you turn off that garden hose this minute. It's making spots on the TV picture tube."

"Leroy did *what* in the swimming pool?"

"Celia! Get your sister off that sofa in that wet diaper."

"Who wanted the peanut butter and catsup sandwich? It's ready."

"Ann, get the phone and tell whoever it is I've run away from home."

"Shut the door!"

"Now you've done it. You've swallowed your space maintainer in your bubble gum."

"When you put meal worms in the refrigerator,

Dan, kindly mark them 'meal worms.' Labeling them 'cole slaw' is not funny.

"Roger. I want to talk with you. Sit down. I've had it with you. You tease the younger kids. You hog all the toys. You refuse to take naps. Mr. Wick and I had a talk about you just last night. If you don't shape up, we're going to send you home to live, do you understand?"

I breathed a sigh of relief, "Thank goodness. Do you realize that for a moment, I thought all of these children were yours?"

Mrs. Wick looked at me numbly, "None of them are mine. Kenny is an only child. Some of these children are lost, strayed, or just plain bored at home. They wander in and just sorta blend with the surroundings. Kenny just said to me one day, 'I hate crowds' and wandered off to your house."

"How did you know where he was?" I asked.

She shrugged, "Saw him pictured with your family on your Christmas card."

"How do things get so confused?" I mused.

"I don't know," she said tiredly, "you just wake up in the morning and mechanically feed anyone who's at the table and you get so busy with the door opening and shutting and little people wandering in and out and water fights and—excuse me (she leaned over to hear a toddler whisper some-

thing in her ear). It seems your son, Bruce, just locked himself in my bathroom. Do you want to talk to him?"

"My son, Bruce? What's he doing here?"

"He's been coming every day since Christmas. It seems Kenny got a fleet of heavy-duty trucks and Bruce is crazy for them. If you want to leave him here, we could use the exemption on our income tax."

"No, I'll take him home," I said.

Later, I lifted the phone to call my husband. "Hey, guess who's coming to dinner? Remember the little kid who looks like your mother?"

The Elusive Washer Repairman

Every woman in the suburbs had a picture of a washer repairman in her billfold and a telephone number.

If, at any time, she spotted one, she was to report it to a central office where they recorded the sighting and tried to track him down. The fast-talking-elusive-repairman was an endangered species. Only five had been sighted in the suburbs during a five-year period.

We had all heard their voices. They said es-

sentially the same thing, "I have you down for Tuesday." What we didn't know was (a) Who was I? (b) Where is down? and (c) What Tuesday?

But like fools, we waited. Every Tuesday, the streets were barren. Cars stood idle in the driveway. Doors were ajar. Some housewives sat on the curb in anticipation of the arrival of the washer repairman.

My washer had been broken for three weeks when I could stand it no longer. I called the washer repair service and said, "I demand you send me a washer repairman."

"Where do you live?" he asked mechanically.

"In Suburban Gems."

"Our serviceman is probably lost. The houses all look alike to us. He'll get to you."

"When?"

"Look, lady, some people have been waiting longer than you and are desperate."

"Do you know what desperate is?" I asked evenly. "Desperate is sending your kids to school in underwear made from broiler foil. Desperate is washing sheets in a double boiler. Don't you understand? I need a repairman."

"I have you down for Tuesday," he said.

On Tuesday, I was talking in the yard with

Helen when suddenly, a few streets away I got a glimpse of a black leather bow tie.

"It's him," I shouted excitedly.

"What are you talking about?" asked Helen.

"A washer repairman. I saw my first washer repairman." I ran to the house to get the picture. "That's him all right," I said smugly. "Blue shirt, black leather bow tie, dark trousers, and a cap with a bill on it. You phone it in. I'm going over and collar him.

"I can't believe it," I said. "A real, live washer repairman right here in my kitchen. Would you mind if I called my neighbor, Helen? She's never seen a washer repairman and she wouldn't spread it around, honest."

"What's wrong with the machine?" he asked gruffly.

"It won't work."

"Anything else?"

"That's it."

"And for that you called me?" He removed the front panel and at that moment started to speak in tongues.

"Your rump bump is nad. Can't pft the snock without trickin the snear."

"That's easy for you to say," I said, "but what's wrong with it?"

"I sad the roughing won't nit sowse you can't snapf the lig if the ffag won't chort."

"That bad?"

"Bad enough to need a raunch ring sloop."

"Is that why it won't spin?" I asked.

"No, the krincop broke and mital values stoffed to the weil ham made it groin."

I felt like I was talking to Professor Corey with a lip full of Novocaine.

"Could you speak a bit more slowly?"

"How old is the zoinc spring?"

"Oh, the machine is three years old."

His eyes rolled back in his head and he shrugged his shoulders, "Whatya smag?"

"Will it live?"

"With a new thircon tube and a blowfest."

"Sir, could you possibly translate all that for me in a simple sentence that I could tell my husband?"

He stood up, wiped grease off his hands and in a voice that would have put Rex Harrison out of work announced, "Seventy-four dollars and thirty-four cents."

"Well, I suppose it will have to be fixed," I shrugged.

"Can't. Your fasack box is a 19689 model."

"Is that bad?"

"It's a discontinued fasack box. Used 'em only

two months. When the smlax csble ghotend the galopian tube, it congested the tubular laxenspiel and the overflowed hose kinked and someone screwed up and FIRE!"

"Let me get this straight. Are you telling me my fasack box catches fire?"

"What's a fasack box?" he asked.

"Whatever my 19689 model is. Are you telling me it's unsafe and I'll have to get a new machine? Well, I won't pay for it."

"Rapf your warranty, lady," he shrugged.

"Where is my warranty?"

"Printed on the bottom side of the washer."

After the washer repairman left, I discovered I had become an instant celebrity. Women all over the neighborhood piled in to ask questions about what a washer repairman looked like.

"I don't see why you didn't just lock the door and keep him here," said Helen.

"Some things are meant to be free," I said.

Trick or Treat . . . Sweetheart

Halloween was my sixteenth favorite holiday.

It rated somewhere between the April 15th In-

come Tax deadline, and a New Year's Eve without a baby sitter.

My husband and I readied for Beggar's Night a full week before. We stored the lawn furniture, brought the garden hose indoors, hid the clothes-line and clothes posts, and dragged the Junglegym set into the garage for safe-keeping.

When we lived in the city, Halloween had been a night for little people to dress up as witches and little clowns, knock timidly at your door, and wait to be identified before you dropped a gingersnap into their little bags.

In the suburbs, Halloween wasn't a holiday. It was a full-scale invasion. Car pools transported herds of children from one plat to another (planes and buses deposited children from as far as three countries away). Greed stations were set up where loot could be emptied and they could start out "fresh." And the beggars themselves were so intimidating that if your "treat" wasn't acceptable you could conceivably lose your health through pain.

The small children usually came between 5 and 5:30 P.M. while it was still daylight. After that the beggars got bigger, the costumes less colorful, and the demands more aggressive.

Opening the door, I confronted a lad over six

feet tall, wearing a mustache, and carrying a shopping bag.

"My goodness," I cooed, "and what's your name?"

"¿Qué?" he shrugged.

"Do I know you?" I asked reaching up to tweak his mustache. The mustache was connected to his face by his own hair.

His partner nudged him. "¿Cuál es su nombre?"

"Manuel," he answered hesitantly. (Good grief, these had come all the way across the border for a bag of caramel corn.)

Next at the door was a twenty-seven-year-old or so wearing a dirty T-shirt, a leather band across his forehead, carrying a pillow case filled with ten-cent candy bars.

"Let's see," I mused, "you are too old for my insurance man and too big for King Kong. I give up."

He blew a giant bubble in my face and juggled his bag impatiently, "I'm Tonto."

"All right, Tonto," I said, "Here's a bright, shiny penny for you."

"Cripes lady," he said, "can you spare this?" (Later, I was to discover Tonto very strong. Tonto bent TV antenna after I gave him his shiny new penny.)

Mentally, I began to draw up a list of rules and

regulations that would give Halloween back to the little children. How do you know when you are too old to go "begging"?

1. You're too old to go begging when your mask tickles your mustache.

2. You're too old when you've figured out the only thing a penny will buy is your weight and you're watching it.

3. You're too old when you drive yourself to the subdivisions.

4. You're too old when you say "thank-you" and your voice is changing.

5. You're too old when you are rapping on the doors and Johnny Carson is signing off.

6. You're too old when you reach over to close your bag and your cigarettes fall out of your pocket.

7. You're too old when you have a sign on your bag that reads, "Personal Checks Accepted."

8. You're too old when the lady of the house turns you on more than the candy apple she just gave you.

Around eleven o'clock I refused to answer the door.

"Why?" asked my husband.

"Because we have run out of treats and when I told the last guy all I had left to give was a bruised

orange, he moistened his lips and said, 'That's what you think, baby.'"

Seconds later, my husband returned from the door, "Quick! Give me some treats."

"I told you I don't have anything left. The refrigerator is cleaned out. So are the snacks. What do you think they would do if you offered them a raw potato?"

He peeked through the curtain and viewed two motorcycle freaks wearing sleeveless leather vests with no shirt and a helmet with a horn coming out of either side. "I think they would turn my nose inside out."

Crawling into the children's bedroom, we felt around in the darkness until we found their little orange trick or treat bags. We grabbed a few handfuls of taffy to appease the motorcycle gang.

Later, crouched in the hallway, the children's bags between us, my husband looked at his watch. "It's 11:30," he said. "Do we dare turn off the porch light?"

"I don't think so," I said tiredly. "It's too risky. The Mintons turned their lights off early last year and a group stole their garage. How much longer do you think we can hold out?"

"I don't know. How much ammunition do we have left?"

My fingers deftly counted out the bubble gum, the miniature candy bars, an apple with a bite out of it, and a few loose pieces of Halloween corn. "With luck, two or three hours."

We both sat up stiffly as the doorbell rang.

"I love you," I said simply without emotion.

"I know," he whispered.

The Identity Crisis

You would have thought with five thousand people living in Suburban Gems that we would have had an identity problem. This was just not true.

As I told my husband, "All you have to do is to reach out to people and the warmth is there."

"I don't have time to socialize," he said. "I work. I cut grass. I watch a little TV and I go to bed so I can get up tomorrow and start all over again."

"And you're missing the entire concept of rural living," I said. "That of getting to know one another on a personal basis. Today is Saturday. Why don't you go down and borrow Lawnsweeper No. 1's charcoal starter for the party we are having this evening?"

"Is he the one next to the pot-bellied stove on the porch?"

"That's Lawnsweeper No. 2 and you know it. Besides, the stove was stolen last Halloween. No, Lawnsweeper No. 1 lives next to the faulty muffler."

"Oh *him*."

"I know, but his wife's nice."

"What's her name?"

"She's the size 18½ with five garbage cans."

"Why didn't you say so. Incidentally, did you invite the guy who saves his anti-freeze each year?"

"Had to. I invited the people with the air conditioner in their bedroom window and they live right next door to one another."

"That would be awkward."

"I only hope they get along with the super liberals."

"What super liberals?"

"The ones who live two blocks over next to the kid who sets fires."

"How do you know they are super liberals?"

"You know that little black jockey statue that has a ring in it to hitch a horse to? They painted him white."

"I remember that. The rhubarb grower had a fit."

"I've never trusted anyone who grows rhubarb."

"Before I go, do you have anything we've borrowed from Lawnsweeper No. 1 and never re-

turned? I'd feel like a fool asking to borrow something that's never been returned."

"You should feel like a fool. He's the one who borrowed our plunger and loaned it to the people with CATS FOR SALE."

"They've had CATS FOR SALE since we lived here. Do you suppose it's the same cat?"

"I feel sorry for the new people who just moved in next door."

"Who are they?"

"The Airstream people. What that little beauty doesn't have in it, they'll never need."

"They must have money."

"Wait until they find out they're wedged in between CATS FOR SALE and the people who let the plastic pool kill their grass."

"I remember him. Met him at a party at the house with the nut who flew the flag on John Wayne's birthday."

"How could you forget them? They own that big Doberman who hides his head in your crotch and you're afraid to move. Speaking of weirdos, got a card from the two-car garage people."

"How did they ever fit a two-car garage on that lot is what I'll never know."

"If you met them personally, you would know. They're pushy."

"I thought so. Where did they go?"

"Went camping with the people with the built-in appliances."

"It figures."

"You'd better get going."

"Hey, I just remembered. You know how you always accuse me of not meeting new people? I met a newcomer last night when I was looking for our newspaper."

"Who is he?"

"Name is Alan Cornwall."

"I'll never remember that. Who is he?"

"The Porsche with the kid who spits on our tires."

"The one who just sprayed the bagworms?"

"That's him."

"Why didn't you say so? I hate name droppers."

CHAPTER FIVE

The Heartbreak
of Psuburbaniasis

The Seven-Inch Plague

In 1946, the suburbs suffered its first plague.

It struck with little warning and attacked the weak, the bored, the vulnerable seeking relief from the monotony. Its name was television and by 1966, it would enslave sixty-two million families.

We fell victims just before Christmas when my husband carried it home to us from the city.

The disease looked harmless enough—a seven-inch screen that looked like a hand mirror. We put it on the bookcase in the living room, got a vanity bench from the bedroom and positioned our eye-

balls 16 inches from the screen where we became mesmerized as a full-grown woman carried on a conversation with two puppets.

Television was a terminal disease that was to spread and worsen, driving people from acute withdrawal to chip-dip attacks.

Because I am basically a strong person, I was able to resist the disease better than most, but my husband's addiction to television grew steadily worse. He became a sports addict who was in a catatonic state twelve months out of every year.

No one would have guessed that his condition would become so hopeless that I would approach a lawyer to have him considered legally dead. The lawyer advised me that due to the legalities this was not an easy thing to do. Just because a man sits in front of a TV set with eyes fixed and no pulse is not enough. He said I would have to keep a log of my husband's behavior over a year's period of time. I began to keep a diary in August.

AUGUST

The fifteenth of this month was visiting day for the children. Waiting for a beer commercial, I lined them up and said stiffly, "Children, this is your father." He offered them a pretzel at the same time watching a beer can dancing with a hot dog. When

we insisted he stand up, the children gasped. They remembered him as a much shorter man.

SEPTEMBER

The set went out today during the Dallas–Los Angeles game. "It could be a tube," I said.

"Shhh . . . and get out of the way. The Cowboys are ready to score."

"No one is ready to score," I said. "You don't understand. The tube is black."

"That's ridiculous. Look at that lateral . . . my God, they've fumbled."

"Just relax. It could be only this channel experiencing temporary . . ."

"Lady, you are going to be temporary if you don't get out of this room and let me watch my game in peace."

I left him sitting in front of the black screen screaming and cheering. Maybe I can talk some sense to him when he is watching the commercial that isn't there.

OCTOBER

Today, our living room was named the first recycling center to be served by a mobile unit. My husband was so engrossed in watching the World Series, he was quite unaware of what was going on.

Television cameras ground away while cub scouts gathered together eight barrels of cans, six barrels of bottles, and 500 pounds of paper.

I pecked my husband on the cheek as I left. He swatted at me and grumbled, "How did that fly get in here?"

NOVEMBER

I am really worried about my husband. On Sunday, he sat in front of the TV set from noon until 10:30 P.M. There was no evidence of breathing. I called our doctor who wheeled in an EKG machine to check the blood supply to his heart.

My husband rallied for a moment when the machine was placed directly in front of him. He bolted upright in his chair, blinked a few times, started fiddling with the knobs and said, "All right, who's been messing around with the antenna?"

DECEMBER

We have found it easier to decorate Daddy than to move him away from the television set.

First, we covered his feet with a simple felt skirt dotted with sequins. Then we hung a candy cane from each ear, and a string of lights around his head. Tonight, we are going to string popcorn and tinsel around his chest.

It's wonderful being a family again.

I'm terribly concerned about what's-his-name. He has watched more bowls this month than the restroom attendant at Kennedy Airport.

He does not eat well. I poked my head through the door today and said, "Have I got a bowl for you!"

"What is it?" he asked, dipping his spoon into it.

"I call it 'Instant Replay.' In it are shredded sports pages, a dozen or so flip tops from beer cans, a few cigarette butts, and a lock of Howard Cosell's hair."

His eyes never left the set as he chewed mechanically. "It needs salt."

I read somewhere man does not live by Curt Gowdy alone.

Tonight, I slid into a nightgown made of Astro-Turf, and sat on the arm of his chair.

"I have a surprise for you," I said huskily.

"Keep it down. Fess Parker is trying to tree a coon."

"What would you say if I told you I had just bought a water bed?"

At first, I thought he didn't hear me. Then he turned slowly. "Are you serious?"

He bounded from his chair, ran to the bedroom and a smile crept across his face. "Are you thinking what I'm thinking?" he asked.

"I hope so," I breathed.

"Now I can stock my own trout."

MARCH

All the green things are coming out this month, except my husband. He is alive (if you call this living) and is being fed intravenously on a diet of basketball, baseball, golf, and hockey.

It has become a game with the family trying to think of ways to get Daddy out of his chair. We have tried, "Your sweater is on fire," "Watching hockey can cause bleeding gums," and "I am leaving. You get custody of the kids."

There is something very unnatural about a man who has a niche in the wall and every day puts fresh flowers under a picture of George Blanda.

APRIL

The baseball strike postponed the opening game thirteen days. Through conscientious throat massage and stuffing his mouth with pebbles, we were able to get my husband up to four words a day during this period.

The first day he said, "Wha . . ."

The second day he said, "What."

The third day he was up to, "Whhhat is yyyour naaaame?"

The players settled their differences soon after and he has regressed once more to clearing his throat.

MAY

We put his mother in knee socks, shin guards, and a hockey face mask and shoved her in front of his chair for Mother's Day.

My husband was watching a ping-pong game and granted her an audience for only a few seconds. Then he punched her playfully on the arm and said, "Hang in there, kid."

JUNE

In an attempt to clean out all of the old things we never use any more, I realized that I had inadvertently set my husband at the curb on top of a rusted bicycle.

The driver of the truck led him to the house and said, "It's cute, but what's it for?"

"It does a lot of things," I said. "It eats leftovers, contributes body heat to a room, and can quote more statistics than the *Sports Almanac*. We use him for a doorstop."

"What's he doing with a candy cane over each ear?"

"He looked so great at Christmas, we hated to take him down."

JULY

"I am leaving you," I said calmly. "I can't stand it any more—the loneliness, the boredom, the roller derbies, the golf tournaments, the snacks. I'm young. I have all my own teeth. I want to see a movie besides the Frazier-Ali fight. I want to dance and drink champagne from a slipper. Do you understand?"

"Shh," he said, "there's a commercial coming up. The one where the beer can dances with the hot dog."

The Suburban Myth

There was a rumor going through the city that the suburban housewife drank her breakfast, accepted obscene phone calls—collect—played musical beds with her neighbors, and rewrote the book on Show and Tell.

The rumor was started by Edward C. Phlegg, the builder of Suburbian Gems who was smart enough

to know that when virtue moves in, there goes the neighborhood. And if anything could sell the suburbs, sin could.

Everyone who lived there had the feeling that everyone was "swinging" except them. In fact, one evening in the paper there was a story about a "local" young mother who put her children under sedation every afternoon and engaged in an affair.

The idea intrigued us and we devoted our entire coffee klatsch to it. "Okay, who's the little temptress who is spiking the peanut butter with Sominex and carrying on in the daylight?"

We all sat there stunned.

"Marci?"

"What!" she sputtered. "And give up my nap?"

"Helen?"

"If you find my car in the driveway and my front door locked, call the police. I have my head in the oven."

"Linda?"

"Get serious. The last time I was in my bathrobe at noon, I had a baby in the morning and was dressed in time to get dinner that evening."

The plain and simple truth is the suburbs were not conducive to affairs. Bus service was lousy and in the winter you couldn't depend on it at all. The house numbers were all fouled up and it was difficult

to find your way through the rows of houses in the plat.

The neighborhood was crawling with preschoolers who insisted on coming into their houses to use the bathroom. The floor plan was clumsy. There were too many traffic areas—too much glass —and besides, there were no alleys for a Plan B alternate exit.

Everything was against us from the beginning, including the domestic rut we had fallen into.

As Marci pointed out, "I think we're fighting a losing battle. We wouldn't recognize a pitch if we heard it. Take me. Please. My vocabulary has been reduced to five sentences which I mumble like a robot every day of my life. They never change.

1. Close the door.

2. Don't talk with food in your mouth.

3. Check out the clothes hamper.

4. I saw you playing with the dog so go wash your hands.

5. You should have gone before you left home.

"The responses never vary—not in ten years of child raising. One night at a party," she related, "I drifted into the kitchen in search of an ice cube when a devastating man leaned over my shoulder and said, 'Hello there, beautiful.'

" 'Close the door,' I said mechanically.

" 'I don't believe we've met,' he progressed. 'My name is Jim and you are ????'

" 'Don't talk with food in your mouth.'

" 'Hey, you're cute. I like a sense of humor. What say we freshen up your drinkypoo and find a nice, quiet spot all to ourselves.'

" 'Check out the clothes hamper,' I said brusquely.

"He hesitated, looking around cautiously, 'Are you putting me on? I mean we aren't on Candid Camera or anything are we?' He slipped his arm around my waist.

" 'I saw you playing with the dog so go wash your hands.'

"His arm dropped and he edged his way to the door. 'Listen, you just stay put,' he said, 'I've got something to attend to.' "

"Tell me you didn't," said Helen.

"I yelled after him, 'You should have gone before you left home.' "

"Did you ever see him again?"

"Never," said Marci sadly.

"Well, someone is having a good time out there," said Linda. "Who could it be?"

"What about that slim blonde in the cul-de-sac, Leslie?"

"What about her?"

"I think she drinks," said Linda.

"What makes you think that?"

"Her curtains are drawn all day, the dog is never out, the car is always there, and she's pale."

We all exchanged glances. "You don't know about Leslie?"

Linda shrugged her shoulders. "She doesn't drink?"

"Not a drop," I said. "She's a Daytime Soap Operaholic."

"You're kidding."

"No, she has a fifteen-serial-a-day habit. Just sits there day in and day out with the curtains drawn and cries."

"Just because you watch a lot of soap operas doesn't mean you're addicted," defended Linda.

"Haven't you seen the literature from SO (Soap Operaholics)? Here, if you have any one of these symptoms, you're in trouble."

Helen handed Linda the SO Handbook.

1. Do you watch a soap opera at seven in the morning just to get you going?

2. Do you watch soap operas alone?

3. Do you hide *TV Guide* so your family won't know how many serials you are watching?

4. Do you lie about how many shows you watch a day?

5. Do you contend you can turn off "As the World Turns" and "Love of Life" any time you want to?

6. When you are "Guiding Light"–ed are you an embarrassment?

7. Do you refuse to admit you're a Soap Opera-holic even though you refused to miss "The Secret Storm" to have your baby?

"If that isn't a kick in the head," said Linda. "The Suburban Orgy is a myth!"

Helen clapped her hand over her mouth. "Lower your voice, you fool. What do you think would be the resale value of these houses if that got out?"

Hosting a Famine

Fat just never caught on in the suburbs like I thought it would. I used to sit around and think how this is the year for the Obese Olympics, or the Pillsbury Eatoff or Bert Parks warbling, "There she goes, Miss North, South, and Central Americas," but it never happened.

Fat just never made it big. No one championed thin more than the women in Suburban Gems. Some dedicated their entire lives searching for a lettuce that tasted like lasagne.

They exercised. They counted calories. They

attended Diet Seminars. Their entire conversation centered around how wonderful it felt to starve to death.

Ever since the babies came I had noticed a deterioration in my own body. My neck became extended, my waist filled in, the hips ballooned, the stomach crested, and my knees grew together.

One day my husband looked at me and said, "Good heavens. Are you aware that you are shaped like a gourd?"

At that moment, I converted to the suburban religion called Cottage Cheese. I ate so much cottage cheese my teeth curdled.

That wasn't the worst of it. Once you were an ordained cottage cheese disciple, you were committed to total understanding of the entire diet community.

I don't think I will ever forget the first luncheon I gave for my neighbors in Suburban Gems. They were all on a different diet. It was like hosting a famine.

Helen was on the Stillman diet which means eight glasses of water, lean meat, and a bathroom of her own. (What does it profit a woman to look thin if you have to wear a nose plug for the rest of your life?)

Ceil was on the Atkins diet for which I cooked

an egg swimming in butter served on a table in the corner due to her acute bad breath. (No diet is perfect.)

Marge was still on the drinking man's diet. She required a bottle, a little ice, and a clean glass. (Marge hadn't lost a pound, but it didn't seem to make any difference to her.)

Ethel was on the Vinegar-Kelp diet. (She worried us. She kept drifting toward the ocean.)

Wilma was enjoying maintenance on her Weight Watchers program. Before dinner was served, she ate the centerpiece (a candle and a plastic banana) and mumbled, "Bless me Jean Nidetch for I have sinned."

I, of course, had my cottage cheese.

Why do women do it?

You're talking to a pro. There was a time when I derived some comfort out of the knowledge that one out of every three Americans is overweight. But I never saw the one. Everywhere I went I was flanked on either side by the two chart-perfect women.

I was surrounded by women whose pleats never separate when they sit down, who wear suspenders to hold up their underwear, who have concave stomachs and the gall to say to me, "I'm cutting down. Do you want my dessert, honey?"

Every dieter has her moment of truth when she faces up to the fact that she is overweight. Sometimes, it's just a little thing like seeing a $50 bill on the sidewalk and not being able to pick it up, or accusing the car wash of shrinking your seat belt, or having shortness of breath when you chew gum. With me, it was a photograph taken on the beach. You couldn't see the blanket I was sitting on, or the sand, and only a small part of the ocean.

My husband said, "The best diet in the world is to put that picture of yourself on the refrigerator door."

He was right. The picture was delicious and actually contained few calories, but with the picture gone I fell into my old eating habits.

The Fat-Picture-on-the-Door diet is just one of many that have swept the country during the past decade, each one promising you more food than you can eat, instant results, and strangers on the bus coming up and asking you to dance.

There was one diet that wasn't publicized, but I think had great merit. It was called the Tall Rat Experiment X-70, or as it was popularly called, "Grow Up—Not Out."

The program was perfected by a scientist named Bert Briarcuff whose basic philosophy was, "There is no such thing as a fat girl. They're only too

short." Of course; why hadn't anyone thought of that! Women weren't overweight. They were undertall.

He gathered together several cages of obese rats and went to work to make them look taller.

The results were astounding. Rats in wedgies looked five pounds thinner than those in loafers. The rats in jump suits with vertical stripes gave the illusion of being thin while those in polka dots looked grossly overweight.

Then he employed the old photographic trick. When a rat was talking with someone in the gutter, the rat placed himself on the curb. If his companion was on the curb, he stood on the steps. If his partner jumped on the steps, he would leap to a spouting above.

Briarcuff found that by teasing the rat's hair, his cheekbones would stand out like Katharine Hepburn's. Women didn't have to starve to death any more. They would just have to learn to create an illusion of tallness.

The Tall Rat Experiment X-70 spread like wildfire in our neighborhood. We shopped at tall girl shops to get the waistlines to hang around our hips. We volunteered to take off our hats at movies. I personally made no new friends over five foot two.

At a dance one night I vowed to dance with no

one taller than I. I bet I danced with every ten-year-old boy there.

After six months, however, the Tall Rat Experiment X-70 began to bore me. I was sick of stacking pillows in the car to make me look like my head was coming through the roof.

Besides, I had a new toy. The kids chipped in and bought me a Flab-Control belt. As they explained it to me, there was no dieting. All I had to do was put the adjustable belt, which was equipped with a small electronic buzzer, around my waist. When my stomach muscles became slack, the buzzer would sound. It was a case of chronic flab. The noise drove me crazy. I went back to cottage cheese.

Desperate, I enrolled in one of the Gastric Show and Tell classes offered at the high school in the evenings.

Their program seemed quite revolutionary to me. Foods that I had always considered decorations for the mantel like carrots, cucumbers, squash, and chard were touted as edibles. Following interesting lectures on nutrition and how certain foods were needed for the body, our instructor, Miss Feeney, asked, "Are there any questions?"

"What if I go through all of this and discover the life after this one is all fat people?"

"Don't make trouble," she said softly. "Just try the foods."

By the end of three weeks when I had not dropped an ounce, Miss Feeney took me aside and said, "You promised you would try to stick to our diet. What happened?"

"Miss Feeney," I said, "you have to face up to what you are dealing with. Dieters are basically nice people. I have a snout full of integrity. I don't throw chewing gum on the sidewalk. I don't put less postage on my letter than I know it takes. And I don't lie about my age. But when it comes to diets, you can't believe a word I say."

"You will live to eat those words," she said.

My face brightened. "Are they fattening?"

Oh, there were others. The denture-adhesive diet where you cement your teeth together and the one-size-fits-all pantyhose worn to the table, but I always came back to cottage cheese.

It's not so bad—a little gravy over it once in awhile, a cottage cheese sandwich between two warm slices of homemade bread, a cottage cheese sundae with a glob of chocolate. . . .

CHAPTER SIX

Ya Got Trouble

NEWS ITEM: Plans for a proposed drive-in movie will be submitted to members of the Suburbian Gems Plat Council at Wednesday night's meeting.

The theater, to be known as The Last Roundup, would be erected on the patch of ground between "CLEAN FILL DIRT WANTED. CALL AFTER 5 P.M. at 959-8800" and Ned Stems' Car Wash. Estimated to occupy about thirty acres, it will feature a western motif, 350 speakers, a refreshment stand, and permanent personal facilities. Prof. Harold Swill, vocal band director of Suburbian Gems High School, is heading a group of dissidents opposing The Last

Roundup and is expected to speak out against the proposal.

"A drive-in movie!"

"Don't you understand? Friends, either you are closing your eyes to a situation you do not wish to acknowledge or you are not aware of the caliber of disaster indicated by the presence of a drive-in movie in your community.

"Well, ya got trouble, my friends, right here, I say trouble right here in Suburbian Gems. Sure, I'm a lover of the arts and certainly mighty proud, I say mighty proud to say it.

"I consider the hours I've spent with Sousa and Romberg are golden, helps you cultivate timing, discipline, a natural ear, and a way to get girls.

"Did you ever take a pocket comb, covered with toilet paper on a picnic and improvise with Tiger Rag—hah! I say any boob can fake a few bars of the "Beer Barrel Polka," but I call that tacky—the first big step on the road to the depths of degrada . . . I say first the Rape of Mozart, then a near-beer six-pack.

"And the next thing you know your son is marching with hair right down to his knees, listening to some stoned-out hippie talking about pot.

"Not a shiny cooking pot with Mom's ham and beans, no siree, but a pot where they freak out of their skulls, makes you sick I should say, now friends let me tell you what I mean, you got R (restricted), X (nothing censored) and a GP where Flipper gets a hickey—movies that make the difference between a pervert and a bum with a capital B that rhymes with D that stands for drive-in.

"And all week long your Suburbian Gems youth'll be goofing off—I say your young men will be goofing—goofing away their noontime, suppertime, choretime too, hook the speaker to the car, never mind getting the lawn fertilized, the sand in the litter box, sitting little sister and never bother delivering the Sunday paper till the supervisor calls on a Sunday afternoon and that's trouble, my friend —lots of trouble—I'm thinking of the kids in the back seat, kissing till their braces spark, cold popcorn, melted ice balls and that's trouble, right here in Suburbian Gems with a capital T which rhymes with D which stands for drive-in.

"Now I know all you folks are the right kind of parents. I'm gonna be perfectly frank. Would you like to know what kind of conversation goes on while they're watchin' those outdoor flicks? They'll

be talkin' about Gatorade, trying out filter tips, popping in breath mints like pill-popping fiends, and bragging all about how they read *Valley of the Dolls* in one swell evening.

"One fine night as they leave the drive-in, headed for the malt shop, you'll find your son, your daughter in the arms of an over-sexed sophomore, mattress-minded—all systems go, parental guidance . . .

"Friends! The idle motor is the devil's playground!

"Trouble, oh ya got trouble, trouble right here in Suburbian Gems, trouble with a capital T that rhymes with D that stands for drive-in. We surely got trouble—gotta figure out a way to stamp out puberty.

"Trouble—trouble—trouble.

"Mothers of Suburbian Gems. Heed the warnings and the telltale signs of corruption before it's too late.

"The minute your son leaves the house, does he stuff his 4-H bylaws in the glove compartment?

"Does he take a blanket on a date and tell you the heater in the car isn't working and it's August?

"Does he have a copy of *Playboy* hidden between the pages of *Boy's Life?*

"Has he ever refused to finish a knock-knock joke in your presence?

"Are certain words creeping into his conversation—words like 'far out' and 'Linda Lovelace' and 'Ma, where's your purse?'

"Well, my friends, you got trouble, trouble with a capital T that rhymes with D that stands for drive-in.

"You surely got trouble, right here in Suburbian Gems, remember God, Motherhood, Flag—and Paul Harvey.

"Oh, oh you got trouble, terrible, terrible trouble that field of passion under a sky of stars is the flag of sin.

"You got trouble, trouble, trouble, oh great big trouble right here in Suburbian Gems with a T that rhymes with D that stands for drive-in."

NEWS ITEM: Plans for a proposed drive-in movie were approved last night when members of the Suburbian Gems Plat Council reached a compromise.

Originally, council members complained that the speakers might contribute to noise pollution in the area. Approximately 140 students, representing Suburbian Gems High School, volunteered as a

group to turn the sound off completely during the showing of movies.

Prof. Harold Swill, band director of Suburbian Gems High School, said, "It is maturity like this that restores my faith in young people."

CHAPTER SEVEN

It Comes with the Territory

Loneliness

No one talked about it a lot, but everyone knew what it was.

It was the day you alphabetized your spices on the spice rack.

Then you dressed all the naked dolls in the house and arranged them on the bed according to size.

You talked to your plants and they fell asleep on you.

It was a condition, and it came with the territory.

I tried to explain it to my neighbor, Helen.

"I'm depressed, Helen," I said, "and I think I

know what it is. (Excuse me) '*Lonnie!* I see you sneaking out of the house with my mixer and I know what you are going to do with it. Put it back!' "

"More coffee?" asked Helen.

"Just a half a cup. I've seen this coming for a long time. The symptoms are all there."

"What symptoms?" asked Helen.

"Helen, I'm so bored. I went to the food locker yesterday to visit my meat."

"You're kidding."

"No. And the other day I flushed a Twinkie down the toilet just to please Jack Lalanne. (Just a minute) 'Is anyone going to get the phone? Never mind. Hello. Yes. What do you want? I'm in therapy with Helen. You'll be home late and don't wait dinner. Right.' Now, where was I, Helen? Oh yes, my behavior. It's bizarre. Remember when a man came out to clean the septic tank? I dropped everything, ran out, and sat on the edge of the hole and asked, 'So, what's new with you?' "

Helen nodded silently.

"I called my mother long distance the other day just to tell her I found a green stamp in my sweeper bag."

Helen stirred her coffee slowly. "Did you ever put up your hair to answer the door?"

"Yes. Oh yes," I said with relief. "Excuse me, Helen, someone's at the door. (Later) It was Joan. She just dropped off her two and she'll be back for lunch. Where was I? Oh yes, my problem. I find myself doing odd things I've never done before. Remember when Dr. Joyce Brothers was on a local talk show and they invited questions from the audience? I called in, Helen. I really did. And I announced to the entire English-speaking world that I wanted her psychological opinion of a man who insisted on sleeping next to the wall. Did I ever tell you that, Helen? Bill refuses to sleep on the outside of a bed. He's positively paranoid about the inside track. Didn't it ever occur to him that just once I might like to sleep next to the wall?"

"Your phone is ringing again," said Helen.

"It was the school nurse. Wanted permission to give my son an aspirin. What he really needs is an enema. I wonder how many people are wandering the streets today in glasses who only need an enema. More coffee?"

"No, I can't stay long," said Helen.

"I've thought about my problem ever since we moved out here and I think I've finally put my finger on it. Every morning, we see the men driving out of paradise onto the freeway and into the city. Leaving us to what? Did I tell you I spent an hour

and a half the other morning putting together a cannon out of balsa wood that I found in the cereal box only to discover one of the kids swallowed the wheel and we couldn't play with it? Wouldn't you know if you had a wheel in your mouth?"

Helen sighed. "You going to the Frisbee recital at the school Friday?"

"I suppose so. Hang on a minute. There goes Nancy and I still wanted to talk with her about Wednesday. 'Hey Nancy! We going to that 1-cent tree sale Friday after the store? Let's go early. It's a mob scene.' Sometimes, Helen, I wonder why we moved to the suburbs. As I told the girls at Trim Gym class last week, I never thought I'd see the day when I'd want my own apartment before the kids did."

"You're just restless," said Helen.

"No! I'm not restless. That's not the word," I said vehemently. "Restless is having lunch with your wigs and having a good time with them. It's a temporary condition that goes away. I'm talking about old, Helen. I'm old. Don't protest. I know what I am. I'm old and fighting for my identity in a young society. Everyone around me is under twenty. My doctor carries a gym bag. Our lawyer is still in braces. And I swear to you my dentist had a string on his mittens last winter. Do you know

what it is to go into a confessional and have your priest reeking of Clearasil?"

"It's not your imagination?"

"It's not my imagination. I don't know what is wrong with me. I'm . . . I'm so desperate. I purposely picked a fight with the hamster yesterday. I stood in front of the hall mirror and said, 'So, who did you expect? Snow White?' "

"There's nothing wrong with the way you look," comforted Helen.

"I'm a mental midget, Helen. My husband is growing professionally every hour and I didn't even know penguins got barnacles on their feet until Pearl Bailey missed it on Hollywood Squares. It's hard to talk to a man who has a meaningful relationship with the TV set."

"Well," said Helen, "I've got to be going."

"Say it! I'm boring, aren't I?"

"Of course you're not boring."

"Do you know that if I had continued my night school classes I would have graduated from college this June. That's right. If I had just found my car keys I could have picked up my B.A. and could be one of those women who only wash on Saturdays and freeze their bread."

Helen looked at me squarely. "Do you know what you are?"

For a moment, there was only the silence of a toilet being flushed consecutively, two dogs chasing one another through the living room, a horn honking in the driveway, a telephone ringing insistently, a neighbor calling her children, the theme of "Gilligan's Island" blaring on the TV set, a competing stereo of John Denver, one child at my feet chewing a hole in the brown-sugar bag, and a loud voice from somewhere screaming, "I'm telling."

"I'm lonely," I said softly.

"Tell your husband," said Helen.

Tell my husband.

I once read a poll of what husbands think their wives do all day long.

The results were rather what you would expect.

Thirty-three percent said women spent five hours out of each day putting lint on their husband's socks.

Twenty-seven percent said they spent four hours daily pouring grease down the sink and watching it harden to give their husbands something to do when they got home.

Ten percent swore their wives held the door open all day to make sure all the warm/cool air (depending on the season) got out of the house.

A walloping 58 percent said women divided their time between hiding from the children, watching

soap operas, drinking coffee, shrinking shirt collars, discarding one sock from every pair in the drawer, lugging power tools out to the sandbox for the kids to play with, and trying to get the chenille creases out of their faces before their husbands came home.

I was dialing Mrs. Craig's number when my husband came home one night after my conversation with Helen.

"Who are you calling?" he asked.

"Mrs. Craig. I thought she could sit with the children for a few days while I ran into the city to visit Mother."

My husband leaned over and gently replaced the receiver. "Do you honestly believe that I can't handle things around here without you? I'll do double time between here and the office and fill in until you get back."

"You've never been a strong man," I said.

"What kind of a crack is that?"

"I'm only suggesting that any man who has to have a spinal block to trim his toenails doesn't have the greatest threshold of pain in the world."

"And who went to bed for three days when she had her ears pierced?"

"That's not true. Look, I was only trying to spare you. Are you sure you can handle things

around here? The kids? The cooking? The laundry? The routine?"

"Does Dean Martin know how to handle a martini?" he grinned. "Of course I can handle this stuff. Don't worry about it. You just go off and do what you have to do and don't give us another thought."

I didn't give them a thought until I let myself into Mother's house in the city. "Call home," she said.

"One quick question," said my husband, "what does 'Bwee, no nah noo' mean?"

"Who said it?"

"Whatya mean who said it? Your baby just said it and looked kinda desperate."

"It means, 'I have to go to the bathroom.' "

"Thanks, that's all I needed to know. Have a good . . ."

"It also means, 'I want a cookie. Where are my coloring books? The dog just crawled into the dryer. There's a policeman at the door. I am floating my $20 orthopedic shoes in the john.' The kid has a limited vocabulary and has to double up."

"I can handle this. It's just that she looks so miserable."

"It also means, 'It's too late for the bathroom.' "

As I readied for bed, the phone rang again.

"What's up?" I asked.

"No problem," he said cheerfully. "It's just that Maxine Miltshire just called and can't drive the car pool tomorrow because she's subbing for Janice Winerob on the bowling team. She can pick up— unless it rains. Her convertible top won't go up. However, if the weather is decent she can pick up and trade with Jo Caldwell who is pregnant and three weeks overdue, but who had a doctor who was weak in math. That means I will drive Thursday unless Jo Caldwell's doctor lucks out. In that case I'll have to call Caroline Seale because I have an early meeting and it might rain. Do you understand any of this?"

"No."

"I'll call you tomorrow night."

The next night I answered the phone. There was a brief silence. Then, "Well, I hope you're happy, Missy. I am now the only thirty-eight-year-old child in my office who has been exposed to Roseola. I was late for work because little Buster Smarts was eating chili off the dashboard of my car and spilled it all over the upholstery and my job is in jeopardy."

"Why is your job in jeopardy?" I asked.

"Because *your* son answered the phone this morning while I was putting catsup on sandwiches

and I heard him tell Mr. Weems, 'Daddy can't come to the phone now. He's hitting the bottle.' "

"Tomorrow is Saturday. It'll be better," I promised.

The phone rang early Saturday.

"Hello," I giggled. "This is Dial-a-Prayer."

"Oh, you're cute," he snarled, "real cute. Just a couple of questions here. First, where are the wheels off the sweeper?"

"On the back of the bicycle in the garage."

"Check. Where does the washer walk to when it walks?"

"It never gets any farther than the door."

"Check. When was the last time you were in the boys' bedroom?"

"When I was looking for eight place settings of my good china."

I arrived home much later from the city than I intended. Everyone was in bed. My husband staggered to the door.

"I'm home," I announced brightly. "Tell me, why is there an X chalked on the side of our house?"

He rubbed his eyes tiredly.

"A baby sitter put it there. I think we're marked for demolition."

I wandered through the house. The dog was drinking out of an ashtray. There was a pad of

blank checks by the phone with messages scribbled on them. The blackboard had a single message on it, "I'm leaving and I'm not coming back." Signed, "Daddy."

"Why is the baby asleep in the bathtub?" I asked.

"She drank four glasses of water just before bedtime."

"There is a crease on your face shaped like a duck."

"I had to separate the boys so I slept in the baby's bed."

I opened up the refrigerator and a leftover reached for me and I slammed the door shut.

"What happened?" I asked, spreading my arms out to make a wide circle.

"Don't start up," he said. "It's all your fault. I had dinner so long in the oven that the bucket caught fire."

"What bucket?"

"The cardboard bucket holding the chicken."

"You're supposed . . ."

"Don't say anything. I mean it. While I was trying to put out the fire, *your* baby chose a rather inopportune time to get a penny stuck up her nose. I've got thirty-five boys in the bathroom watching movies. I tried to make a drink and there are no ice cubes, and besides, Maxine called to tell me I've

been named homeroom mother! And all the while you are living it up at your mother's, drinking out of clean glasses."

"You'll feel better after a good night's sleep," I said as he crawled back into the crib.

I was right. The next morning he turned to me brightly and said, "Good-bye dear. You'll find everything in ship-shape order. Boys, kiss your father good-bye."

The boys turned away and one said flatly, "He murdered our guppies."

"We'll talk about it tonight," he said. Then he whispered, "By the way, could you call and let me know how Lisa makes out on 'As the World Turns'?"

The Pampered Dog

When the dogs in the city talked among themselves, the conversation always drifted to the suburbs.

It was the dream of every canine to someday live out where every dog had his own tree, where bad breath had been conquered, and where fleas had to register at the city limits and carry their I.D.'s at all times.

The suburban dog had it made. Owners pampered them to death with dietary dog food, dental appointments, knitted stoles to take off the evening chill, dog beds shaped like hearts, doggie bar nibbles, and car seats.

I personally felt I could live a fulfilled life without a live-in lawn fertilizer, but my husband convinced me the children would grow up to steal hubcaps without the security and affection of a dog.

In a weak moment, we bought Arlo.

The first day Arlo came home, his feet never touched the floor. In a single day he was fed eight times, burped five, danced on the TV set, slid down the banister, was given a bath, blown dry with my hair dryer, visited twelve homes, rode on a bicycle, and barked long distance on the phone to Grandma. He slept his first night under my dual-control thermal blanket.

On the second day, Arlo continued to reign. It took eight saucepans to warm his dinner, he watched a puppet show staged by the children for his benefit and as he headed for the door, one of the children slapped his brother while the third child leaped for the dog and opened the door . . . first.

On the third day, there were some complaints from the children that Arlo had kept them awake all

night with his howling. When I suggested the dog be fed, one son said his brother did it, who vowed his sister did it, who said, "It's not my turn."

On the fourth day, my daughter took Arlo to Show and Tell. He blew it by showing too much and didn't have a finish, and a clean-up committee of one was delegated to do the honors. One of the children said if Arlo followed him to school one more time and he had to bring him home he was going to kick him.

On the fifth day I reminded all of them that the rule of the house was that the first one to spot a puddle, etc., automatically cleaned it up. The entire household fell victim to indoor blindness.

On the sixth day, I said, "Has anyone seen Arlo?"

One of the children yelled back, "Arlo who?"

So much for security and affection.

I began to become suspicious that Arlo was not a registered Irish Setter when his roots came in white, his nose was concave, and within six weeks he was eye level to the kitchen table.

This was confirmed as I sat in the vet's office one afternoon. I shifted uncomfortably as a woman read a magazine to a cat with running eyes, a pet raccoon ran around the playpen, and a small terrier mistook my leg for a forest.

Finally, a well-dressed man on my left with a small poodle ventured, "I am intrigued with your breed. What kind of a dog is that?"

"Irish Setter," I said.

He looked astounded, "You have papers?"

"All over the house." I got a firmer grip on the forty feet of pink plastic clothesline around Arlo's neck and ventured, "What's wrong with your dog?"

He looked soulfully at the poodle and patted it gently, "Jessamyn isn't sleeping well."

"Me either," I said.

"She's just been through a rather bad pregnancy."

"Me too," I said excitedly.

"Actually, Jessamyn is too highly bred and tense for motherhood."

"I know what you mean," I commiserated.

"We thought of aborting, but there was so much social pressure brought to bear, we finally consulted a psychiatrist who thought it best to go through with the births and then get them away from her as soon as possible so she could pull herself and her life together again and then exercise some measure of birth control. What's wrong with your . . . Setter?"

"Worms."

"How disgusting," he said, wrinkling his nose. "I

wonder what's keeping that vet?" he said. "I have some flowers in the car for Jessamyn's mother."

"Jessamyn's mother?" I asked, my eyes widening.

"She's (he leaned over and spelled slowly) P-A-S-S-E-D-O-V-E-R. Jessamyn and I go once a month to visit. They were very close. She's at the Bow Wow Cemetery. Beautiful grounds. Incidentally, if you ever go on a vacation and need a reliable shelter the K-9 Country Club is a marv. Restricted, you know. None of your tacky clientele. The ones with the new luggage. They have a chef there you wouldn't believe. Well," he said as he was summoned, "Nice meeting you and good luck to—what's-his-name?"

"Arlo."

"Oh my God," he said, touching his nose with his linen handkerchief and sniffing.

Because I am basically a "swift" person, it didn't take me long to realize that Arlo and I were to become an "item." Just the two of us. I fed him, kept his water bowl filled, got him shots, license, fought fleas, took out ticks, and let him in and out of the house, 2,672 times a day.

My husband came home one evening to view the dishes on the breakfast table with hardened egg, the unmade beds, the papers from the night before strewn all over the living room, the laundry spilling

out over the clothes hamper onto the floor, and said, "Fess up! You've been playing with that dog all day long."

"Did anyone ever tell you you have a future in comedy . . . along with Jane Fonda and Eric Sevareid?"

"C'mon now," he teased, "look at the way that little dickens is jumping up and down."

"The little dickens is aiming for your throat. He wants out."

"Don't be ridiculous," he said. "He just came in when I did."

"So now he wants out. I go through this over two thousand times a day. The dog has a Door Wish. He can't go by one without scratching it until it opens. The other day he scratched, barked, and jumped for fifteen minutes. Finally, I opened the door and he ran in and two minutes later started scratching again. He realized he was under the sink."

"Why does he want out so much? Maybe something is wrong with his kidneys?"

"A dog with kidneys the size of a lentil could have better control than he has."

"I got it," said my husband, snapping his finger. "We'll go out when he goes in. That way we'll confuse him into not knowing if he's out or in."

Standing there huddled in the darkness on the cold porch scratching with our paws to get in, I tried to figure out where I went wrong. I think it was when my mother said to me, "You're not getting any younger."

"You are going to think this is a dumb question," I asked, "but why did we get a dog in the first place? I mean, if it was for the kids, forget it. All it has done for them is to keep them from looking down when they walk."

My husband took me by the shoulders and I saw shock written on his face. "Do you mean to tell me you really don't know?" he asked.

"No."

"We did it for you," he said.

"You bought a dog for me?" I asked numbly.

"But of course. For your protection. Maybe you don't realize the dangers of being by yourself out here in this wilderness. There are loonies and crazies running around all over the place."

"True, but we're all on a first-name basis."

"You may be as light about it as you like, but just wait until some day when I am at work in the city, and a wild-eyed stranger knocks at your door and wants to use your phone on some pretense and you'll be mighty thankful Arlo is around."

I looked at Arlo. He was lying on his back in

front of the fireplace with all four paws sticking up in the air—passing gas.

The mental picture of a sex pervert at my door and the only thing between us was Arlo, sent a shiver down my spine.

It was several weeks later that Arlo was to be put to the test. I answered the door to find two men standing there rubbing Arlo behind the ears.

"Pardon us," said one of the men, "but our truck broke down and we'd like to phone our company for help."

I grabbed Arlo by the collar and jerked him to his feet. "I must apologize for the dog," I said. "I'll try to hold him so he won't tear you to shreds. Down boy!"

The men looked at one another and shrugged as the dog blinked sleepily and slumped to the floor. "He looks pretty friendly to me," said one of them.

I knelt and pushed back Arlo's lip to show his teeth. When I released the lip, it fell back into a ripple as he licked my hand. "You may not believe this but I had to register this dog with the police as a deadly weapon. Just ask anyone around here and they'll tell you about Arlo."

"Arlo?" the men grinned.

"Steady boy!" I said, propping him up to get him

off my foot. "Just don't make any sudden moves," I cautioned.

One of the men came inside to use the phone while Arlo and I held the other man at bay at the door.

"Why, one of the kids was just playing around one day," I related nervously, "and inadvertently punched me on the arm. Arlo liked to have made raw meat out of him before we could pull him off."

"Is that right?" asked the stranger.

His friend returned and together they thanked me, playfully pushed Arlo over on his back, scratched his stomach, and left.

As they walked to the car I heard one say, "Boy, that was one terrifying experience."

"What, the dog?"

"No, the woman. She's a real whacko!"

They were probably right and I realized things weren't going to get any better when one afternoon I answered the phone. It was Mr. Wainscott.

"Remember me?" he asked. "I'm Jessamyn's father."

"Of course," I said, "from the vet's waiting room. Jessamyn is the one who had the same symptoms as I had. I've been dying to ask what the doctor prescribed."

"Lots of bed rest, time to herself, no major decisions, analysis, and a light social calendar."

"I guess one out of five isn't bad," I said. "So, how are things?"

"Fine. I was calling to ask if Arlo could attend Jessamyn's birthday party. Are you there?"

"Yes," I said. "A birthday party. Where?"

"This Saturday at two. We live two blocks north of the highway next to the golf course. You can't miss it. Oh, and it's informal."

When we arrived a dozen or so dogs romped around the room.

"So glad you could come," said Mr. Wainscott.

"I must apologize for the present," I said. "Arlo ate it on the way over."

"That's perfectly all right. Gang!" he shouted, "this is Arlo. Arlo is one of Jessamyn's neighbors. Don't be frightened," he said as Arlo stood at the sink and licked water out of the spigot. "He's big for nine months. Why don't you pick Arlo up in a few hours?"

I don't know what happened to Arlo at the party, but he was never the same dog after that. One day I caught him looking at his teeth in the bathroom mirror. (Jessamyn had her teeth capped). Another time, he hopped on the bathroom scale, gasped, and

refused to eat table scraps any more. One afternoon, I begged Arlo for ten minutes to go outside. He was sitting in a chair watching David Susskind.

The only time he seemed happy was in his encounter group.

The Garage Sale

There are four things that are overrated in this country: hot chicken soup, sex, the FBI, and parking'your car in your garage.

What's such a big deal about pulling your car into a garage if you have to exit by threading your body through an open window, hang from a lawn spreader, climb over the roof, and slide down a garden hose before reaching the door.

Our garage was a twilight zone for garbage, the dog, old papers, boxes, excess laundry, redeemable bottles, and "projects" too awkward (big, dirty, stinking) to have in the house. So was everyone else's. In fact, there was a garage clause in most of our accident polices that if we were folded, bent, spindled or mutilated while walking through our garage we could not file a claim.

Then one day something happened to change all of that. Helen came over so excited she could

barely speak. "How would you like to go to a garage sale?" she asked.

"I have one."

"You don't buy the garage, you ninny," she said. "That's where the sale is. A woman over in the Dreamland Casita plat just advertised and I want to check it out."

A good fifteen blocks away from the sale, we saw the cars bumper to bumper. I had not seen such a mob since the fire drill at the Health Spa.

We parked the car and walked, slowly absorbing the carnival before our eyes. On the lawn, a woman was trying on a skirt over her slacks. "Do you do alterations?" she yelled to the woman who had sold it to her.

"Whatya want for 25 cents?" she yelled back, "an audience with Edith Head?"

Inside, mad, crazy, frenzied ladies fought over an empty anti-freeze can for $1.50 and an ice cube tray with a hole in the bottom of it for 55 cents.

One lady was lifting the snow tires off the family car and shouting, "How much?" Another was clutching a hula hoop over her shoulder and asking, "Are you sure this is an antique?" An older couple was haggling over a pole lamp insisting it would not fit into their car, and arrangements must be made for a suitable delivery date. It was marked 35 cents.

Outside, Helen and I leaned against a tree. "Can you believe this?" I asked. "I feel like I have just attended Alice's tea party."

"What did you buy?" asked Helen excitedly.

"Don't be ridiculous," I said. "It's all a bunch of junk no one wants. I didn't see anything in there I couldn't live without."

"What's that under your sweater?"

"Oh this. It's the only decent thing worth carrying out."

I held it up. A framed picture of the "Last Supper" done in bottle caps.

"Isn't that exquisite?" I asked.

"That is without a doubt the worst looking picture I have ever seen. Look how distorted the faces are and besides, Judas is rusting. How much did you pay for it?"

"Six dollars," I said defensively.

"*Six bucks!*" said Helen doubling over, "you've got to be kidding." As she laughed, an electric iron dropped from behind her handbag.

"What's that?" I asked.

"An iron. I really needed an extra one."

"It doesn't have a handle."

"So why do you think I got it for 75 cents?"

"Look," said a lady who had been standing at our elbow for ten minutes, "are you going to buy

this tree or just stake it out so no one else can get to it?"

"No," I stammered . . . moving away.

She dug her shovel into the soil and began moving dirt.

Frankly, I didn't give the garage sale another thought until another neighbor, Grace, said to me one day, "Why don't you stage a garage sale?"

"Because spreading one's personal wares out in a garage for public exhibition is not only crass, it smacks of being tacky."

"Pauline Favor made eighteen bucks," she said.

"Get the card table," I snapped.

My husband was less than enthusiastic. "Those things are like a circus," he said. "Besides, we need all of this stuff."

"Hah!" I said, "that is all you know. This stuff is junk. One of these days we'll wake up and find the junk has taken over. We won't be able to move for boxes of rain-soaked Halloween masks, and stacks of boots with one missing from each pair, and a broken down potty chair. If you want to live like a pack rat, that's your business, but I've got to make a path through this junk—and soon."

In desperation, he gave in and the garage sale was scheduled for Thursday from 9 A.M. to 5 P.M.

At 6:30 A.M. a woman with a face like a ferret

pecked on my kitchen window and said, "I'll give you 30 cents for this door stop."

I informed her the doorstop was my husband who is not too swift in the mornings and if she didn't put him down this instant, I would summon the police.

By 7:30 there were fifteen cars parked in the driveway, nineteen on the lawn, two blocking traffic in the center of the street, and a Volkswagen trying to parallel park between the two andirons in my living room fireplace.

At 9 A.M. I opened the garage door and was immediately trampled to death. Grace said she had never seen anything like it.

They grabbed, pawed, sifted through, examined, and tried out anything that wasn't nailed down, but *they weren't buying.*

"What's the matter with them?" I asked.

"It's your junk. It's priced too high."

"Too high!" I exclaimed. "These heirlooms? Do you honestly think that $8 is too much for a box of candle stubs? And this stack of boots for $5 each. They don't make rubber like that any more. And besides, who is going to notice if you're wearing a pair that don't match? Dare to be different. And take this potty chair . . ."

"For twelve bucks, *you* take it," said a potential pigeon. "You can buy a new one for $15."

I wanted to hit her. "With training wheels? Why, this potty chair can take a kid right into football season. When collapsed, it will fit snugly in an Army duffle bag. It's not for everybody. Only the discerning shopper."

"You are going to have to lower your prices," whispered Grace.

Grace was right. Of course, but she should have prepared me for the personality change I was about to experience when I sold my first piece of junk.

I became a woman possessed. As one by one the items disappeared from the card tables and the nails on the side of the garage, I could not stand to see the people leave.

They bought the boots with a hole in the sole, electric toothbrushes with a short in them, a phonograph that turned counter-clockwise, and an underground booklet listing the grades of Harvard Medical School graduates 1927–1949.

The junk began to clear out and I knew what I must do to keep them there. Running into the house, I grabbed dishes out of the cupboards, clothes out of the closets, and books off the shelves.

I snatched my husband's new electric drill and marked it $3. I ripped the phone off the wall and sold it for $1.75. When my son came home from school, I yanked him off his bicycle and sold it for $5.

I grabbed a woman by the throat and said, "Want to buy a fur coat for $1? I was going to give it to my sister, but she looks like a tub in it."

"I am your sister," she said dryly.

To be perfectly honest, I lost control. Grace had to physically restrain me from pricing the baby who was being admired by a customer who cooed, "I'd like to take you home with me."

It was seven o'clock before the last car left the driveway. I was exhausted mentally and physically.

"Did I do all right?" I asked Grace.

She hesitated, "In a year or two, when you are well again, we'll talk about today."

"I don't know what happened to me," I said.

"You were a little excited."

"Are you trying to tell me I went crazy?"

"I am trying to tell you it was wrong to sell your garbage for 40 cents."

"But she insisted," I said.

"By the way," said Grace, "what's that under your arm? You bought something."

"It's nothing," I hedged.

She snatched the package and opened it. "It's your laundry!" she said, "that you keep in a plastic bag in the refrigerator. How much did you pay for this?"

"Two dollars," I said, "but some of it still fits."

CHAPTER EIGHT

Law and Order

THE TEN MOST UNWANTED WOMEN
IN THE SHOPPING-CENTER PARKING LOT

Dolores Fronkbinder
Throws body over
parking space to save it
for a friend

Debbie Frump
leaves motor running
giving false hope she
is ever coming back

Iris Stigmatism
Pulls into "handicapped only"
parking spot with infected
hangnail

Wilma Whiplash
parks between two spaces
to keep door from getting
dented

Alicia Early
Parks in spot near
door when shopping center
is under construction and
leaves it there

Who's Watching the Vacant House? Everyone.

I had only met Officer Beekman on two occasions.

The first time was when I inadvertently rammed into my husband's car when I backed out of the driveway and he was summoned by my husband. (The case is still pending.)

The second time was when he helped me over a rather bad spot in my driver's test by chalking a B on the brake pedal and an A on the accelerator.

"I suppose you are wondering why I have summoned you," I said as I let him in the front door.

"Yes Ma'am," he said, removing his crash helmet and his dark glasses.

"My husband and I are going on vacation and . . ."

He held up his hand for silence and looked around him anxiously. "Are we alone?"

"I think so."

"Fine. That is the first rule. Never tell anyone you are leaving."

"I understand."

"We handle hundreds of house-watching assignments each year and the key word is: *secrecy*."

"Don't people become sorta suspicious when they see a police cruiser in front of the house every night?"

"I don't park in front of the house every night," he explained, "I just sorta cruise by and give it this." (His head jerked like he was having a neck spasm.) "Now, the second key word is *lived in*. Make your potential burglar believe you are home by leaving on a light or a radio playing. If you'll just tell me where you are going, when you'll be back, and give me a number where you can be reached, we'll take care of everything."

"That's wonderful," I said, seeing him to the door. As he climbed into the car I shouted, "See you in two weeks!"

He touched his finger to his lips and said, "Remember, secrecy is the key word."

Helen was the first one over after he pulled away. "Why was the police cruiser in your driveway?"

"Shhh," I said, looking around. "We're all going to Yuuck Village for two weeks and Officer Beekman is going to watch our house to see that no one burglarizes it. Don't tell anyone. He said the key word is secrecy."

For a change, my husband agreed. "That is the smartest thing you have ever done," he said. "Who are you calling?"

"Officer Beekman's second suggestion was that the house look 'lived-in.' I'm calling Margo to tell her when we are leaving so she can come in every night and turn on a different light. Then I have to call the paper boys and the dry cleaner—and the postman."

"What about discontinuing the milkman?"

"Discontinue the milkman? Why don't you just stand out in front of the house in your underwear and hold up a sign reading, 'COME IN AND BROWSE.' Thieves follow milkmen like flies follow a garbage truck. Let me handle this. I'll just have him deliver four quarts every other day like he's always done."

"Won't the crooks get suspicious when he drinks

all four quarts and takes the empties back to his truck?"

"He'll just rattle a few bottles and pretend he's delivering," I sighed. "Now, where was I? Oh yes, I have to tell Mike we're leaving so he can come over and cut the grass, and Mark so he can plant garbage in our cans and put them at the curb on garbage day and . . ."

"I don't believe this," said my husband.

"You'd believe Maybelle Martin, wouldn't you? She and Dave were going to Disneyland for a few days. She dressed up her sewing form in a pants suit and a wig and propped it against the mantel with a drink in its hand. Her house was robbed the next morning. They took almost everything but the form. Do you know what gave her away?"

"Someone noticed she had a pole for legs?"

"The ice cubes in her drink melted and even crooks know no one stands around with a warm drink in his hand."

"You have told seven people already that we are leaving. How many more are you going to tell?"

"Well, I have to tell Charmaine to bring her children over to play in the yard, and Frederika said to call when we leave so she can bring her dog over on a weekend to bark. Naturally, I'll have to

call my hairdresser, my cleaning lady, my insurance agent, my car pool girls . . ."

"That's sixteen."

"My Avon lady, AAA, the soft-water man, the utility meter reader, the Cub pack . . ."

"That's thirty-three."

"Of course our family vet and the check-out girls at Willard's market, my foot doctor, the guys at Bufford's service station, our minister and Miss Baker, who does that chatty column in the *Tattler* . . ."

"Roughly, how many people are you telling we are leaving town?"

"About 683."

"Why don't you just take an ad in *The New York Times?*"

"Glad you reminded me. Grace said a great way to get phones calls while you are gone is to put an ad in the paper selling a toaster or something.

"Or you might even let a dozen insurance agents think you are in need of a good liability policy. There is nothing like a ringing telephone to scare robbers away from an empty house."

"I think you are overreacting to the entire situation," said my husband. "All these elaborate measures to make the house look lived-in are insane. If

you get any more people running in and out of here, we'll have to stay home and park cars."

We both dropped the subject until a few days ago when my husband came into the kitchen where I was preparing dinner. "I met an interesting fellow today in the garage where I park my car," he said. "He arrived here two days ago from Chicago. When I introduced myself he said, 'Oh, you're the fellow who is going to Yuuck Village for ten days beginning the fifteenth of next month.'"

"How could he have known that?" I asked, my mouth falling open.

"It seems his wife's nephew had a corn removed by a foot doctor who attended a cookout the other night at the home of our meter reader."

"Gas, electric, water, or taxi?" I asked carefully.

"It's not that important," he continued. "What was rather interesting was a story he told me regarding their vacation last summer. He said they were only gone a matter of hours when their house was ransacked. Picked clean."

"Didn't I tell you!" I shouted triumphantly. "Let me guess. They forgot to leave a radio playing low so burglars would hear sound. Or they didn't hire a cat to sit in their window. I got it. They didn't plan a party in their house while they were gone or leave bicycles lying around the driveway."

"They did all of those things," my husband said softly.

"Then what did they forget?" I shouted.

"To lock the front door."

Suburban Gems Police Blotter

- Stolen grocery cart spotted

- Dog complaint

- Fire hydrant buried by snow

- Officer requested for women of the moose law enforcement appreciation dinner

- Summons issued for DWI, driving with 0.10 percent or more alcohol in bloodstream and illegally parking in lobby of drive-in bank

- Woman having trouble with neighbors

- Rescue unit answered call of cat in dryer

- Went to gas up police car and pump went dry

- Report of strange-acting car. It was running well

- Call from supermarket that young male trying to purchase beer for his sister to shampoo hair

- Found door open at town hall. Nothing missing

- Woman reports harassing telephone calls from ex-husband

- Owner of dog in heat demands thirty dogs be evicted from his property

- Had brakes and drums replaced on police car

- Young boy hitchhiking claims he was running away from home. Sought assistance in crossing highway

- Bread delivery tipped over on sidewalk. Notified store manager. Restacked bread

- Report of septic tank odors

- Checked out burgled car wash coin box

- Got police car washed

- Woman reported car lights in cemetery. All three cruisers responded to call

- Women reported large dog from next door deposited a mound the size of Mt. Olympus on their lawn each morning. Requests gun permit

- Man reports having trouble with house builder. Thinks wife may have been harassed. His attorney working on problem

- Bicycle stolen while chained to bike rack

- Supermarket reports bike rack stolen

- Restaurant files missing report for twelve steaks and five bottles of booze. Possibly party in progress

- Flat tire on police car fixed at garage

- Illegal burning of leaves at 8486 N. Platinum Lane

- Bad check returned to woman who thought her husband had made deposit

- Fire gutted Suburbian Gems library. Loss estimated at $143.95

- Subject observed urinating in parking lot

- Man reports kid plugging flow of creek

- Principal holding suspected drug user. Subject revealed pills to be breath mints

- Private citizen complains churchgoers blocking his driveway every Sunday. Warned of legalities in letting air out of tires

- Officer requested to speak to Rotary Club on "Crime! It's a jungle out there!"

- Officer called to investigate dirty word scratched on exit ramp freeway sign. Sign out of jurisdiction. Also misspelled

- Expectant mother requested assistance in getting out of compact car

CHAPTER NINE

Put Your Winnebagos into a Circle and Fight!

You couldn't help but envy the Merediths.

Every weekend, they left their all-electric, three-bedroom, two-bath, w/w carpeted home with the refrigeration and enclosed patio and headed for Trailer City.

Here, these thrill-seekers parked their trailer between a tent holding thirty-five people, and a public toilet. They did their laundry in a double boiler, cooked over an inverted coffee can, killed mosquitoes that had their own air force, and watched the sun set over a line of wet sleeping bags.

We never dreamt that someday we too could escape all of our conveniences and head beyond the suburbs where the air smelled like kerosene and the streams were paved with discarded beer cans.

Then one day my husband pulled into the driveway with a twenty-one-foot trailer hooked behind the car.

It was the biggest thing that had happened in the neighborhood since home milk deliveries. The entire neighborhood turned out to inspect it.

Standing in the middle of the trailer, I felt like Tom Thumb. It looked like a miniature doll house. Those dear little cupboards. The little beds. The little stove. The miniature doors and windows. The tiny closets. What fun it would be keeping house. Of course, there would have to be a place for everything and everything would have to be in its place, but I could hardly wait to hit the open road.

"You know," said my husband, "it might be even more fun if we went with another family."

"You're right," I said. "Things are much better when they are shared."

"Are you thinking about the same couple as I am thinking?"

"Get serious," I said. "Who else would I be thinking of but Eunice and Lester?"

Eunice and Lester had moved to Suburbian Gems

the same time as we. Their two children were between our three agewise and there had never been a cross word between us.

"Lester is a prince," said my husband. "Why I'd use Lester's wet toothbrush."

"And I've never had a sister closer to me than Eunice," I mused. "If Eunice was pregnant, I'd volunteer to carry it for her."

We called Eunice and Lester that night and together we planned a two-week vacation. Originally, we talked about the first of June but Lester had an appointment to have his teeth cleaned and he needed a few days to get back on his feet and Eunice's horoscope forbade her to travel until her sign got off the cusp, so we juggled the schedule around and came up with the first two weeks of July.

The *Mayflower* never had a bigger send-off. The four of us packed provisions for three months. There were Eunice's astrology charts and her wok ("I never go anywhere without my wok"), and Lester's pills and ointments and of course the gear brought by their children Beezie and Wendyo: a four-by-six baseball return net and an inflated walrus (which when we tried to deflate threw Wendyo into terminal paranoia), the food and the extra linens, and the motor for the boat—but it was fun.

Then we all waved good-bye and climbed into the wagon and were off. "Isn't this going to be fun?" I said, clasping Eunice around the waist.

"Watch it!" she winced. "My kidneys."

"What's wrong with your kidneys?" I asked.

"Nothing, now that your son has his guitar out of them."

"Maybe we should trade," I giggled. "I'll take my son's guitar out of your kidneys if you take your son's bubble gum out of my left eyelash."

We both laughed so hard we almost fell out of the car.

Several miles out of town a pattern began to form. Our two families and our little travel trailer were only part of a caravan of campers which snaked in a thin line all the way across the United States.

At one point, we tried to pass a motorcycle, which was attached to a U-Haul, which was pulled by a trailer, which was hooked to a boat, which was hitched to a Volkswagen, which was being towed by a station wagon laden with vacationers.

They were all winding around the highways looking for the same thing—a picnic table. Hours passed and everywhere we went it was the same story. Someone had gotten there first. I looked at the children. Their faces were white with dust, one

was coughing from exhaust fumes, and the others were staring silently with hollow, vacant eyes out of the rear window.

"Maybe," I said, touching my husband's arm gently, "we should turn back. We should never have left the suburbs to come to this God-forsaken scenic route. It's not for myself, I'm begging, but —for the children. Soon they are going to need fresh air . . . fresh fruit . . . restrooms . . ."

"Just hang on a little longer," said my husband. "I heard at the last pit stop there was a picnic area about eight miles down the road."

"Do you suppose it would have a shade tree nearby?" I asked. "Don't get your hopes built up," he said. "It was just a rumor."

We bumped along another ten miles when Eunice spotted it. "Look! A picnic table!"

Tears welled in my eyes. "All right, children, get ready. The moment the car slows down, you all jump out and run over and throw your bodies across the table until we can park and get there."

They poised their bodies at the door ready to spring when panic set in.

"There's an Airstream coming in at four o'clock," said Lester.

"There's also a four-wheel drive bearing down over the ridge," said my husband, shifting gears.

We all skidded in in a cloud of dust as the children spilled out of the cars and flung themselves on the table. When the dust had settled, we discovered we had all been too late. A dog was tied to the picnic table to stake it out for another camper.

We pulled our vehicles into a circle to plan our next strategy.

Somehow, after a dusty lunch standing around a gas pump, we all felt better and continued on toward the Ho Hum Campgrounds, arriving around dusk.

"Parking the trailer is a little tricky," said my husband. "I'd appreciate a little help."

"What are fellow-campers for?" said Lester. "I'll direct you from the front."

"And I'll stand near your left rear wheel," chirped Eunice.

"I'll stand near your right rear wheel," I said, saluting smartly, "and the children can relay any messages you can't hear."

My husband pulled up and started to back in.

"Turn your wheels," yelled Lester.

"Which way?" answered my husband.

"That way!" said Lester.

"What way is that way?" returned my husband.

"To the left," said Lester.

"Your left or my left."

"Your left."

"Hold it!" screamed Eunice.

"What's the matter?" yelled my husband, jamming on the brakes.

"Not you," yelled Eunice, "*him!*"

"Who me?" yelled Lester.

"No, Beezie. He's making those faces at Wendyo again and . . ."

"For crying out loud, Eunice," snapped Lester. "This is no time to yell at the kids."

"Okay, when Wendyo cries, I'll send her to you."

"What did I just hit?" yelled my husband.

"Just a tree limb," I shouted.

"I can't see. It's on my windshield."

"You should have been watching for him above," said Eunice.

"It wasn't my side, sweetie," I purred.

"Turn! Turn!" shouted Eunice.

"Which way?"

"The right way."

"Not right," yelled Lester. "She means left."

"Don't speak for me, Lester," said Eunice, "I can speak for myself."

"Are we level?" asked my husband.

"What's this little hole for?" I asked.

"Where is it?" asked my husband.

"Right here in front of me," I said.

"I mean *where* is it?"

"Under your tire."

"Good heavens, that's my hook-up."

"Straighten it up," said Lester.

"Pull forward," said Eunice, "you've only got this far."

"How far?" asked my husband.

"Look at my hands," said Eunice.

"I can't see your hands," said my husband.

"I can see them," said Lester, "and she's crazy. You got another three feet back there."

"Let's just leave it," said the driver, "until it stops raining."

"It's not raining," said Lester, "you just hit a water hook-up on the next trailer."

"My God," I groaned as the water hit me, "and me without a hairdresser for two weeks."

"Moooommmmmeeeee," whined Wendyo.

"Did I tell you, Lester?" (To Wendyo:) "Tell your father."

"What is she doing out of the car?" yelled Lester.

"If you get your foot run over don't come skipping to me, Missy."

"Dad! If Wendyo is out of the car, how come we can't get out?"

"I think we're in quicksand," I yelled. "The car and the trailer are sinking."

"It is not sinking," said Lester. "The tire is going flat."

My husband got out of the car. It had taken nine people and forty minutes to help him back into a spot that was a pull-in . . . accessible by two roads.

The next morning, we all felt better about our togetherness—so much so that I decided to keep a diary.

THE FIRST DAY: This is going to be such fun. All of us have a job on the duty roster. The children are in charge of firewood. Lester is the camp doctor. Bill is in charge of camp maintenance, and I am the house mother. Eunice is the social director and is picking out songs to sing around the campfire.

The men are having a wonderful time. As Bill said this morning, "That Lester is a prince. Do you know what he is doing? He is out there fixing the motor already."

"What's wrong with the motor?" I asked.

"The pin dropped out of it in 12 feet of water at the dock."

"Who dropped it?"

"Lester did, but it was an accident. He reached

back to swat a mosquito and lost his balance. Lester said he had a balancing problem."

I can believe that.

THE SECOND DAY: As Eunice was out on a nature hike with the children (they are labeling trees) Bill said, "What are you doing?"

"Washing out the public garbage cans," I said. "As Eunice pointed out, you don't know where they've been. She is so meticulous. You know, we are so lucky. Can you imagine spending two weeks with a couple of slobs? Yuuuck."

THE FIFTH DAY: Didn't mean to miss so many entries in my diary, but I've been so busy. Isn't it funny, the things you worry about never happen. I was wondering how two cooks could occupy this little kitchen. Eunice hasn't been in the kitchen but once since the night we got here. It's not her fault. Poor dear has been trying to find a store in the area that stocks bean curd cakes and lotus roots for the wok.

Lester is a klutz. I don't know how poor Eunice stands it. Always running around with a nasal spray hanging from his nostril. Right after he dropped the pin from our motor in the water, he dropped our flashlight down the only outdoor convenience. It's still down there lit. Now we can't see where we're going—only where we've been.

I have to tell myself fifteen times a day that Lester was wounded at Ft. Dix when he stapled his elbow to a private's request for transfer.

THE SIXTH DAY: What kind of animals leave hair in a brush on the kitchen table? At first, I thought it was little Beezie or Wendyo but neither of them has combed his hair in a week. It has to be their parents.

Tonight, just to break the monotony, we invited the Parkers over from the next trailer to spend the evening. Eunice told that amusing story she tells about the nun not knowing what to order in the bar and having a little booze in a coffee cup. I love the way she tells it. Eunice *is* funny. Her horoscope told her she was going to have an adventure on water. I hope so. I've carried every drop of it!

THE NINTH DAY: This trailer is driving me up the wall. There's more room in an oxygen tent and it's better arranged. The other day I took the cap off the toothpaste and had to open the window.

The refrigerator holds a three-hours' supply of meat, the oven makes one piece of toast at a time, the sink converts to a bed, the bucket doubles as a bar stool, and yesterday when Lester and Eunice slept late, we had breakfast on Lester's chest.

Tonight, Eunice sleeps with the wok!

THE ELEVENTH DAY: As I said to Bill when we

undressed for bed, "How long have we known Eunice and Lester?" He said, "About six years," and I said, "Isn't it strange that we never noticed that Lester snorts when he laughs. When Eunice told that ethnic slur about the nun again, he sounded like a '38 pickup truck with water in the fuel line."

"He's a prince though," said my husband. "I mean the oil slick wasn't really his fault. He was only trying to wash the dust from our car by backing it into the lake and just accidentally hit the crankcase with a rock. It would never have happened had he not had one of his blinding migraines."

THE TWELFTH DAY: Are you ready for this? King Lester said this evening. "Why didn't you tell us the mosquitoes were so bad this time of year?"

"If Eunice had gotten off her cusp in June, there wouldn't have been any mosquitoes," I said. "Besides, my kids have taken all they're going to take from Heckle and Jeckle or whatever you call your two weak chins with the overbite."

"It's not the season," said Eunice bitterly. "It's the fact that your children are on the threshold of puberty and still don't know how to close a door."

"Speaking of doors," I said, "when was the last time you opened an oven, refrigerator, or cupboard door?"

"I suppose my braised prawn sandwiches did not meet with your middle-class taste?" she snarled.

"I don't pretend to be a connoisseur of *bait!*"

"Just a second, Erma," interrupted Lester, "if it hadn't been for Eunice's wok, we'd have starved to death."

"Only because you used my only large cooking pan to store a snapping turtle for Sneezy."

"That's Beezie!"

"It's one of the seven dwarfs!"

"Someone had to play with the children," said Lester, "since Bill was too busy cleaning out his tackle box."

"Only after you spilled the suntan lotion all over the lures, Fat Fingers."

"Hold it!" I said. "We are all exhausted from having such a good time. Let's sleep on it."

THE THIRTEENTH DAY: Tomorrow we go home. No more marshmallows catching fire and burning black. No more sand in the butter. No more bathing suits that smell like fish. No more soggy crackers.

All that is left is a stack of postcards no one mailed.

You know something? Now that I've read them, I didn't realize we had such a good time.

I wonder if Eunice and Lester could get off her cusp for a couple of weeks next year. . . .

PRESENTED TO: *Estelle*

YOU ARE AWARDED THIS SUPERMOM
CERTIFICATE

1. Because: you have a pencil by
the telephone.
2. you see the DENTIST twice a year.
3. you grow your own HERBS.
4. you make the CHILDRENS' clothes.

CHAPTER TEN

Super Mom!

A group of first-graders at Ruby Elementary school were asked by their teacher to draw a portrait of their mother as they saw her.

The art was displayed at an open house.

Some mothers were depicted standing on a sailboat. Others were hauling groceries, cutting grass, or talking on the telephone.

All the mothers had one thing in common. They were pregnant.

In the suburbs, pregnancy wasn't a condition, it was the current style. Everyone was wearing a

stomach in various stages of development—whether you looked good in one or not.

I frankly felt I was too short for pregnancy and told my husband so. A lot of women looked great when they were expecting. I was always the one with the hem that reached down to the ankle in the back and up to the knees in front and I forever dribbled things down my stomach. Usually, I went into maternity clothes at two weeks and by the ninth or tenth or eleventh month my drawstrings wouldn't draw and my mirror talked back to me.

Sometimes, I'd sink into a chair in my fifth month and couldn't get out until the ninth month of labor/or the chair caught fire—whichever came first.

The preoccupation with motherhood was the only thing we had in common. From then on, mothers were divided into two distinct groups: the Super Moms and the Interim Mothers.

The Super Moms were faster than a speeding bullet, more powerful than a harsh laxative, and able to leap six shopping carts on double stamp day. She was a drag for all seasons.

Super Mom was the product of isolation, a husband who was rarely home, Helen Gurley Brown, and a clean-oven wish. There was a waiting list for canonization.

The Interim Mothers were just biding their time until the children were grown. They never gave their right name at PTA meetings, hid candy under the dish towel so the kids would never find it, had newspapers lining the cupboard shelves that read, "MALARIA STOPS WORK ON THE CANAL," and secretly believed that someday they would be kissed by an ugly meter reader and turned into Joey Heatherton.

There were no restrictions in Suburban Gems. Super Moms were free to integrate at any time they wished and when one moved in across the street, I felt the only decent thing to do was welcome her to the neighborhood.

The moving van hadn't been gone a minute when we saw her in the yard waxing her garden hose. I walked over with my nine-bean "trash" salad and knocked on the door. Her name was Estelle. I could not believe the inside of her house. The furniture was shining and in place, the mirrors and pictures were hung, there was not a cardboard box in sight, the books were on the shelves, there were fresh flowers on the kitchen table, and she had an iron tablet in her hand ready to pop into her mouth.

"I know things are an absolute mess on moving day," I fumbled.

"Are people ever settled?" she asked, picking a piece of lint off the refrigerator.

Then she waltzed in the children and seeing one lock of hair in her son's eyes, grimaced and said, "Boys will be boys!"

If my kids looked that good I'd have sold them.

"Hey, if you need anything from the store, I go every three hours," I offered.

"I shop once a month," she said. "I find I save money that way by buying in quantity and by planning my meals. Besides, I'm a miser with my time. I read voraciously—right now I'm into Cather and I try to go three or four places a week with the children. They're very aware of contemporary art. Now they're starting the romantics. Could I get you something?" she asked softly. "I just baked a chiffon cake."

I felt my face break out.

"The doctor said I have to put on some weight and I try desperately . . . I really do."

I wanted to smack her right across the mouth.

Frankly, what it boiled down to was this: Could a woman who dyed all her household linens black to save time, find happiness with a woman who actually had a baby picture of her last child?

The Interim Mothers tried to get along with Estelle, but it wasn't easy. There was just no getting ahead of her. If the Blessed Mother had called

Estelle and said, "Guess what, Estelle, I'm expecting a savior," Estelle would have said, "Me too."

She cut the grass, baked her own bread, shoveled the driveway, grew her own herbs, made the children's clothes, altered her husband's suits, played the organ at church, planned the vacation, paid the bills, was on three telephone committees, five car pools, two boards, took her garden hose in during the winter, took her ironing board down every week, stocked the freezer with sides of beef, made her own Christmas cards, voted in every election, saw her dentist twice a year, assisted in the delivery of her dog's puppies, melted down old candles, saved the anti-freeze, and had a pencil by her telephone.

"Where is Estelle?" asked Helen as she dropped by one day.

"Who knows? Probably painting her varicose veins with crayolas to make them look like textured stockings. I tell you that woman gets on my nerves."

"She is a bit much," said Helen.

"A bit much! Would you trust a woman who always knows where her car keys are?"

"I think she'd like to be your friend."

"It wouldn't work."

"You could try."

"You don't know what you are saying. She's

so . . . so organized. They're the only house on the block that has fire drills. Take the other day, the school called to tell her Kevin had been hurt. Do you remember what happened when the school called me when my son flunked his eye test?"

"You became hysterical and had to be put under sedation."

"Right. Not Estelle. She calmly got her car keys off the hook, threw a coordinated sweater over her coordinated slacks, put the dinner in the oven on warm, picked up that pencil by the phone, wrote a note, went to school to pick up Kevin, and drove him to the emergency ward."

"So—you could have done that."

"I'm not finished. In the emergency ward, she deposited Kevin, remembered his birth date, his father's name, and recited their hospitalization number from *memory*."

"I remember when you took Andy to the hospital."

"I don't want to talk about it."

"What was it again the doctor said?"

"He wanted to treat my cracked heels."

"That's right. And you had to write a check for a dime to make a phone call."

"Okay. I remember."

Actually, Estelle didn't bother anyone. She

wasn't much more than a blur . . . whipping in and out of the driveway each day. I was surprised when she appeared at my mailbox. "Erma," she asked, "what's wrong with me?"

"Nothing," I hedged. "Why?"

"Be honest with me. I don't fit into the neighborhood. Why?"

"I don't know how to explain it," I faltered. "It's just that . . . you're the type of woman you'd call from the drugstore and ask what you use for your irregularities."

"All I want is to be someone's friend."

"I know you do, Estelle, and I'd like to help you, but first, you have to understand what a friend is."

"Tell me."

"It's sorta hard to understand. But a friend doesn't go on a diet when you are fat. A friend never defends a husband who gets his wife an electric skillet for her birthday by saying, 'At least, he's not one to carouse around at night.'

"A friend will tell you she saw your old boyfriend—and he's a priest.

"A friend will babysit your children when they are contagious.

"A friend when asked what you think of a home permanent will lie. A friend will threaten to kill

anyone who tries to come into the fitting room when you are trying on bathing suits. But most of all, a friend will not make each minute of every day count and screw it up for the rest of us."

From then on, Estelle, neighborhood Super Mom, began to change. Not all at once. But week by week, we saw her learning how to compromise with herself. At first, it was little things like buying a deodorant that wasn't on sale and scraping the list of emergency numbers off the phone with her fingernail.

One morning, one of her children knocked on my door and asked to use our bathroom. He said his mommy locked him out.

The next week, Estelle ran out of gas while making the Girl Scout run. A few days later, she forgot to tie her garbage cans together and the dogs dragged TV dinner boxes all over her lawn for the world to see.

You could almost see her image beginning to crumble. She dropped in unexpectedly one afternoon and leaned over the divider to confide, "I have come to the conclusion there is an after-life."

"An after-life?"

"Right. I think life goes on after the children are grown."

"Who told you that?"

"I read it on a vitamin label."

"What are you trying to say, Estelle?"

"I am trying to tell you that I am going to run away from home. Back to the city. There's a life for me back there."

"Don't talk crazy," I said.

"I've tried to be so perfect," she sobbed.

"I know. I know."

At that moment, one of Estelle's children ran excitedly into the room. "Mommy! Mommy!" she said wildly, "I was on the side using a toothpaste with fluoride and I only have one cavity."

Estelle looked at her silently for a full minute then said, "Who cares?"

She was one of us.

CHAPTER ELEVEN

The Volunteer Brigade

Crossword Puzzle

ACROSS

14   nine-letter word syn. with frozen dinners, pin in children's underwear, laundry in refrigerator, five-hour meetings, no pay, no health benefits, causing head to hurt a lot.

DOWN

3   six-letter word meaning same as nine across

ANSWER

```
        P
        I
        G
VOLUNTEER
        O
        N
```

"I Am Your Playground Supervisor"

One evening, the phone rang and a voice said simply, "We have not received your response to the mimeographed request that we sent home with your son."

"What request is that?"

"We need you for playground duty at the school."

"Please," I begged, "don't ask."

"Is this the woman who protested paid potties in airport restrooms by throwing her body across the coin slot?"

"You don't understand," I said.

"The woman who made Christmas tree centerpieces out of toilet tissue spindles and macaroni?"

"Don't . . ." I sobbed.

"Is this the freedom fighter who kept them from building a dairy bar in front of the pet cemetery with a flashing sign that read, CUSTARD'S LAST STAND UNTIL THE FREEWAY?"

"I'm only human," I sobbed. "I'll report Monday to talk about it."

On Monday, I met with Mrs. Rush, the homeroom mother. "Mrs. Rush," I began, "there are several reasons why I cannot volunteer for playground duty, not the least being I have not had my shots."

"Your old ones are good for three years," she said mechanically.

"I see. Then I must tell you the truth. I am expecting a baby."

"When?"

"As soon as my husband gets home."

"Do you have any more excuses?" she asked dryly.

"Yes. I'm a registered pacifist."

She shook her head.

"How about, 'I'm a typhoid carrier'?"

"I'm afraid all those excuses have been used before," she said. "Do you realize that only four mothers returned their mimeographed bottoms?"

"That many?" I asked incredulously.

"One mother is unlisted, one had a transportation problem, and the third one was a bleeder. We couldn't take the chance. That left you. Here is a mimeographed page of instructions. You will report Monday and good luck."

Slowly, I unfolded the yellow, mimeographed sheet. It had a picture of a mother with the countenance of St. Francis of Assisi. At her feet were a group of little adoring children. A bird was perched on her shoulder. I smiled hesitantly. Maybe playground duty wasn't the hazard the women rumored it to be.

The first day I opened up my mimeographed page of instructions:

"PLAYGROUND DUTY CONSISTS OF STROLLING AMONG THE CHILDREN AND WATCHING OUT FOR FAIR PLAY."

A group of boys parted and I began to stroll. I felt like a stoolie strolling through San Quentin between Edward G. Robinson and Humphrey Bogart.

"What are we playing today?" I asked cheerfully.

"Keepaway," they chanted, as they tossed an object over my head.

"Boys! Boys!" I admonished. "Put Miss Manieson down. She's only a sub and doesn't understand how

rough little boys can play. If you want to play keepaway, I suggest you use a ball. Come on now, I mean it. I'll give you two minutes to find her glasses and return her to her classroom."

"We don't have a ball," they whined.

"Perhaps these nice boys here could share," I suggested.

"You touch that ball," said a boy who looked thirty-five years old, "and you'll wish you hadn't."

"Look," I said, returning to the boys, "why don't all of you play a quiet game. Let's ask this little fella over here what he's playing. He's sitting there so quiet."

"He's quiet because an eighth-grader just tied his hands behind his back and took his lunch money!" said a small, blond kid. "Who wants to play Rip-off?"

On Tuesday, I went to the principal, unfolded my mimeographed sheet and said, "I should like to talk about rule no. 2: Here, A FIRST-AID CLINIC IS MAINTAINED IN THE SCHOOL FOR CUTS, BRUISES AND OTHER MINOR ACCIDENTS."

"What seems to be the problem?" she asked.

"I feel they really should have some provisions for the kids too."

"We'll discuss it," she said coldly.

Wednesday was one of the coldest days in the

year and I figured there would be few children on the playground. I was wrong. "Boys! Boys!" I shouted, "you must not push or shove. It says right here on my mimeographed sheet, 'SHOVING AND UNDUE PUSHING IS NOT PERMITTED.'"

"We're not shoving and pushing," they said, "we are keeping warm."

"If you keep any warmer, I will have to suspend you from the playground for three days."

"Who says?"

"My mimeographed orders say, that's who. Read this: 'A PLAYGROUND SUPERVISOR'S ORDERS ARE TO BE OBEYED THE SAME AS THE TEACHER'S.'"

He wiped his brow. "You had me worried there for a minute."

"Is it my imagination." I said, "or do I sense you have done something with Miss Manieson?"

"She's only a sub," they grinned.

"Today's sub is tomorrow's birth-control militant," I reminded.

"So, who are you to tell us what to do?"

"I am your playground supervisor," I said, squaring my shoulders.

"So?"

"So, how would you like to go to a nice school where they make license plates?"

"And how would you like to go . . ."

I grabbed my mimeographed sheet out of my pocket, and read, "A PLAYGROUND SUPERVISOR SHOULD DRESS SENSIBLY. SHE NEVER KNOWS WHICH AREA SHE WILL BE ASSIGNED NEXT."

As I read the lips of the class bully, I had the feeling I was dressed too warmly for where I had been ordered to go.

Wanda Wentworth; Schoolbus Driver

Wanda Wentworth has been retired for about ten years now, but they talk about her still.

No one commanded the entire respect of the suburban populace more than Wanda Wentworth who held the record for driving a schoolbus longer than any other woman in the entire school district . . . six weeks.

Every morning, fearless Wanda crawled into a schoolbus and dared do what few other adults would attempt: turn her back on eighty school children.

In the beginning, it had been a job for men only. Strong men who could drive with one hand and pull a kid in off the rearview mirror with the other. Who knew that Robbie Farnsworth could disguise

his voice as a siren and liked to kill a little time by pulling the bus over to the side of the road. Who could break up a fight between two kids with bad bananas.

And then, along came Wanda. She had read an ad for drivers in the *Tattler:*

WANTED

DRIVERS FOR SCHOOLBUS

SEE MAGNIFICENT SUNRISES AND SUNSETS

ENJOY THE LAUGHTER OF CHILDREN AT PLAY

BE A FULFILLED VOLUNTEER

ORPHANS PREFERRED

Few of us saw much of Wanda after she took the job. I saw her only twice: one day in the dentist's office (she had fallen asleep in the chair) and another time in the supermarket when I got a bad wheel and she whipped out her tool kit and fixed it.

"How are things going on the bus?" I asked.

"Terrific!" she said. "There's nothing to it. You just have to be strict. Let them know you mean business."

I looked at Wanda closely. Her right eye rolled around in her head—independently of her left one.

"I don't allow no cooking on the bus," she said, "even when they have a note from home. Now, I know a lot of drivers who don't mind small fires, but I say if you want a hot meal, put it in a thermos."

"I think you are absolutely right," I said slowly.

"Another thing," she said, spitting on her hair and trying to get a curl to stay in the middle of her forehead, "all notes from home have to be legit. They come up with all kinds of stuff. 'Please let Debbie off at the malt shop. Eric is spending the night at Mark's house. Wait for Lillie. She has to get Marci's nail polish out of her locker.' Any time I see a note written on stationery with a pencil or a pen, I know it's a fake. Mothers only write with yellow crayons on napkins."

"You are very wise."

"They're not dealing with any dummy," she said. "Like games. I don't allow any games on the bus."

"You mean they're not allowed to play count the cow or whip out an Old Maid deck?"

"Nope. They get too excited. We tried playing Blind Man's Bluff one day and those little devils spun me around so fast I nearly hit a tree with my bus. I just laid it on them after that. Absolutely no more blindfolding me while the bus was in motion. Actually, the time goes pretty fast," she said, folding

her lower lip into a crescent and biting on it with her teeth until it bled. "By the time I pick them up and they punch everyone on the bus, and open their lunches and eat them, and make their homework into gliders and sail them out of the window, and open the emergency exit in traffic, and take off their boots and leave them under the seats, and unravel the mittens their mothers put on them, and yell obscenities at the motorists passing by, we are at school."

"It sounds like it really has its rewards," I smiled nervously.

"Oh it does. Did you hear that Tim Galloway won first prize in the science fair? He rides my bus. As a matter of fact he constructed a weather station using parts he stole off my dashboard while I was having the bus 'gassed up.' "

"That's wonderful," I smiled, "but I still don't know how you hung on for six weeks. That's longer than any other person in the history of the school. How did you do it?"

"These little gems," she said, patting a bottle of pills in her coat pocket.

"Tranquilizers?" I asked.

"Birth control," she smiled, swatting at a fly that wasn't there.

220

Ralph Corlis, The Coach Who Played to Lose

In the annals of Little League baseball, there was only one man who made it to the Baseball Hall of Shame five seasons in a row. That was Ralph Corlis.

Ralph was an enigma in suburban sports. He brought his two sons to a housing development two years after his wife died, and together they hacked out a life for themselves. They planted a little garden, built a little racing car in the garage, and on a summer evening would go over to the ballfield and watch the kids play ball under the lights.

It was after the third or fourth game that Ralph began to take note of the thirty or forty kids on the bench who wore the uniform, but who rarely played the game.

"What do those kids do?" Ralph asked his sons.

"They watch the team play ball."

"For that they have to get dressed up in full uniform?"

"Oh no," said his son, "they go to all the practices, work out, run, field, catch, pitch, and do everything the team does . . . except play."

Ralph thought a lot about the bench warmers and

one day he approached several of them and said, "How would you like to join my team?"

When Ralph was finished, he had enough for five teams and sixteen benches. The first night they met on a piece of farmland donated by a farmer.

"This is first base," said Coach Corlis, dropping his car seat cushion on the ground, "and this is second," he continued, dropping his jacket, "and I see there's already a third base."

"But . . . it's a pile of dung," said one of his players.

"So, don't slide," said Ralph.

"Do you want to see me pitch?" asked a tall, lean, athletic boy.

"No," said Ralph. Then turning to a kid two feet tall who could scarcely hold the ball in his hand, he said, "You pitch today."

At random he assigned a catcher, basemen, infield and outfield, and said, "The rest of you—relax. On this team, everyone plays."

You cannot imagine what an impact a team where "everyone plays" had on the community. Word spread like a brush fire.

One night Coach Corlis answered his door to discover a visit from three other coaches.

"Hey, what a surprise," said Ralph. "Come in."

"What's your game?" asked one of the coaches.

"Baseball," said Ralph.

"You know what we mean," said one of the other men. "What are you trying to prove? Playing every boy who goes out for the team. How many games have you won?"

"I haven't won any," said Ralph. "I didn't think that was very important."

"What are you, some kind of a loonie? Why would you play a game, if not to win?"

"To have a good time," grinned Ralph. "You should have been there the other night when Todd Milhaus slid into third."

"Unfortunately, losers don't draw crowds," smirked the third coach.

"Oh, we don't want crowds," said Ralph. "Adults just mess things up for the kids. I heard at one of your games that a mother threw a pop bottle at her own son."

"And he deserved it," said the first coach. "He should have had his eye on second base. That kid has the brain of a dead sponge."

"He's pitching for me tomorrow," said Ralph.

"Look," said the second coach, "why don't you let the boys go? What do you want with them? They're not even winning."

Ralph thought a minute then said, "It's hard to explain, but kids go all through their lives learning how to win, but no one ever teaches them how to lose."

"Let's get out of here, Bert," said the third coach.

"Wait a minute," said Ralph. "Just think about it. Most kids don't know how to handle defeat. They fall apart. It's important to know how to lose because you do a lot of it when you grow up. You have to have perspective—how to know what is important to lose and what isn't important."

"And that's why you lose?"

"Oh no. We lose because we're too busy having a good time to play good ball."

"You can't talk sense to a man who won't even sell hotdogs at a game and make 13 cents off each dog."

Ralph Corlis's team racked up an 0-38 record the very first season. The next year, it was an even better 0-43. Parents would have given their right arms to watch the team play, but they were not permitted to view a game.

All eighty of the players used to congregate at a drive-in root beer stand and giggle about their contest. When there was criticism it was from themselves. The important thing was that *everyone was sweating*.

In the annals of sandlot baseball, there had never been another team like it. They had lost every game they played and they did it without uniforms, hotdogs, parents, practice, cheerleaders, lighted scoreboards, and press coverage.

Then one afternoon something happened. Ralph had a little nervous bedwetter on the mound who had never played anything but electric football. He wore glasses two inches thick and refused to take the bicycle clamp off his pantleg.

The kid pitched out of his mind, throwing them out at first, catching an infield pop-up and pitching curves like he invented them.

Ralph's team (it had no name) won the game 9-0.

The boys were strangely quiet as they walked slowly off the field. Defeat they could handle—winning was something else. Ralph sat in his car a long time before putting his key into the ignition. He wanted time to think.

"See you next week, Coach," yelled a couple of the boys.

But Ralph Corlis never went near the cornfield or a baseball game again. As he explained to his sons, "I couldn't stand the pressure."

Confessions of an Officer in the Girl Scout Cookie Corps

No one was more surprised than I at being named Girl Scout Cookie Captain.

I had been in the restroom at the time of the promotion.

The moment following the announcement was rather exhilarating. Mothers crowding around me patting me on the back and whispering in my ear, "If you need anything, I'm in the book," and assuring me, "This is going to be the best year ever."

Then they were gone.

And there were twenty-five little girls looking at me to lead them into door-to-door combat.

"At ease," I said, "you may chew gum if you like."

One girl blew a bubble the size of a pink gall bladder. Another one looked at her watch and shifted her weight to the other foot. The others just stared.

"Now then," I said, "I think this is going to be a great experience for all of us. I'll help you and you can help me. I have only one question before

you leave today. What's a Girl Scout Cookie Captain?"

"She sells cookies," said the girl with the gum.

"And where does she get the cookies?" I asked.

She shrugged, "From her own living room."

I nodded. "I see, and how do they get to her living room?"

"A big truck dumps them there," said another scout.

"Okay, girls, I'll get it all together and be in touch."

At home, I grabbed the phone book and began calling all of those wonderful people who had volunteered to help.

Frankly, I didn't realize there were so many of life's losers in one neighborhood.

"I'd love to help, but I'm allergic to children."

"We're only a one-phone family."

"Give me a break! I'm on a diet and I'm in remission."

"I'm volunteering so much now my husband reported me missing."

"Do I know you? Oh, *that* sister!"

The first meeting of the Girl Scout cookie army went well. We discussed on what day we would take orders and on what day they must report their sales to me. I, in turn, would process the order for the entire troop and then there was nothing left

to do but sit around and wait for C-Day to arrive.

It was about five weeks later when my husband nudged me out of a sound sleep one morning and said, "Do you hear something?"

"Ummm. What's it sound like?"

"Like a truck in our driveway."

We staggered to the window. By the headlights I saw them: full-grown men unloading carton after carton of cookies. "Where do you want them, lady?" they shouted.

I pointed to the living room.

When I told the girls the cookies were in they did a fantastic job of holding their emotions in restraint.

One cried, "There goes the skating party."

Another one slammed down her purse and said, "I wish I were dead."

And another one declared, "If it rains, I'm not delivering."

"It's all right, girls," I smiled, "don't hold back. You can show your excitement if you want to. Frankly, I'm just as choked up as you are. As I was telling my husband this morning as we breakfasted over 250 cartons of vanilla creams, 'This will show me to go to the restroom before I leave home.'"

The delivery of the cookies was a lot slower than I had anticipated. Hardly a day went by that I wasn't on the phone trying to contact one of the girls to pick up their cookies and deliver them.

"Hello, Marcia? I have the eighty-six boxes of cookies you ordered and . . ."

"My grandmother died."

"I'm sorry about that Marcia, but there are still the cookies."

"She was down for twenty-eight boxes."

"I see. Do you happen to know where I can get in touch with Debbie?"

"She moved."

"Where?"

"I promised I wouldn't tell you."

"What about Joanne?"

"She's dropped scouting. She's selling peanut brittle for the band now."

"Marcia! You tell the girls I'm up to my Girl Scout motto in cookies and I want them out of my living room by this weekend, do you hear?"

"Have you tried freezing them?" she asked mechanically.

"Freezing them! Sara Lee should have such a freezer!"

Stripping a captain of his rank in the cookie crops is not a pretty sight. I ripped off my armband, turned in the sign from my window that read "COOKIE HEADQUARTERS" and laid my golden badge on top of my yellow scarf.

"Do you have your records book?" asked the leader.

"I do," I said smartly. "It's all there. There are

143 cartons of cookies unaccounted for and $234 or $12.08 outstanding. It's hard to tell."

"Do you have anything to say."

"Yes," I said, my voice faltering. "I want the record to show that I tried. When twenty-five girls literally vanished from the earth, I tried to dispose of the cookies myself. I sprinkled cookie crumbs on my salads, rolled them into pie crusts, coated pork chops in them, and packed them in lunches. I made paste out of them and mended books, rubbed them on my callouses and rough elbows, and wedged them under the door to keep it open.

"I sent them out with my bills each month, wore two of them as earrings, gave them as wedding gifts, and set glasses on them and pretended they were coasters.

"I put them under my pillow for good luck, made an abstract for the living room, dumped a canful over my compost and crumbled some of them up for kitty litter. I have a cookie rash on 97 percent of my body."

"Is that all?" asked the leader somberly.

"Yes, I'm finished."

As I started to leave the room, I could hear nominations being presented for next year's cookie captain.

I turned suddenly and took a front row seat. I couldn't take the chance of leaving the room again.

CHAPTER TWELVE

"By God, We're Going to Be a Close-knit Family If I Have to Chain You to the Bed!"

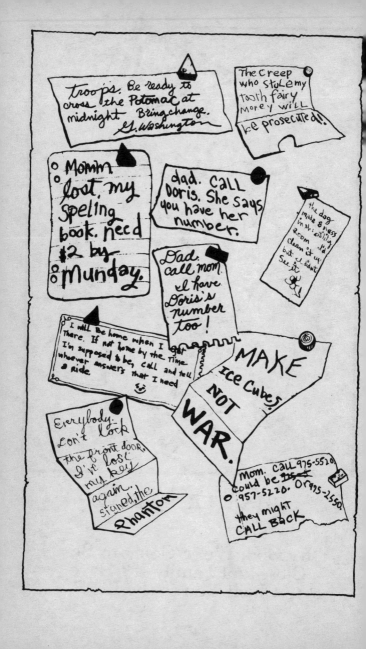

The Frozen Kiosk

When historians poke through the rubble of the suburban civilization, they will undoubtedly ponder the refrigerator mystique.

For no apparent reason, other than its functional value, the refrigerator became the meeting place of the American suburban family. It also became a frozen message center whereby anyone could drop by anytime of the day or night.

The rules of communications via refrigerator were simple: Don't write with food in your hand. If phone numbers were illegible, be a sport. Mes-

sages left unclaimed over seven years would be destroyed.

This, then, is how the suburban family communicated:

THE LANGUAGE OF REFRIGERATOR DOOR

"*Momm. Lost my spelling book. Need $2 by Munday.*"

"*Dad. Call Doris. She says you have her number.*"

"*Dad. Call Mom. I have Doris's number too!*"

"*I will be home when I get there. If not home by the time I'm supposed to be, call and tell whoever answers that I need a ride.*" Unsigned.

"*Everybody. Don't lock the front door. I've lost my key again. Signed, the Phantom.*"

"MAKE ICE CUBES. NOT WAR."

"*The dog made a mess in the utility room. I'd clean it up but I didn't see it.*"

"*Mom. Call 975-5520. Could be 957-5220. Or 975-2550. They might call back.*"

"*The creep who stole my tooth fairy money will be prosecuted!*"

"Troops. Be ready to cross the Potomac at midnight. Bring change. G. Washington."

"Mom and Dad: How much is it worth to you for me to lose the notice of PTA Open House?"

Starving to Death at the Spiritual Family Feast

I got the idea from a sermon.

In church one Sunday, the Reverend said, "The dinner table each evening should have all the elements of a service . . . a spiritual family feast whereby each one can share his day and his love with one another.

"Wasn't that beautiful?" I said in the car on the way home.

"Mom! Guess who stole the sponge out of the Holy Water font?"

"I'm telling. You know when we're supposed to shake hands in a sign of peace? Guess who pressed a dirty nose tissue in my hands then wouldn't take it back?"

"If one of you kids doesn't stop kicking the back of my seat," said their father, "I'm going to clear the car."

235

"Will you knock it off?" I said. "Didn't anyone hear the sermon?"

"Yeah, it was something about sharing pizza."

"It was not about sharing pizza. It was sharing your spiritual love at a family feast."

"Same thing."

"Do you know when was the last time this family ate a meal together?"

No one spoke.

"It was four years ago at Grandma's birthday."

"I remember," said our son, "I did the dishes that night."

"You did not," said his sister, "I did them because I remember we had lasagna that stuck to the pan and I had to soak it."

"Yeah, for three weeks!"

"Well, I'm not like some people who put a giant bowl in the refrigerator with a peach pit in it."

"Only because you eat everything in sight . . . including the pits."

"Look," I said, "we are long overdue. Tomorrow night, this entire family is going to sit down together and eat a meal. Only a certificate of death —a recent one—will be acceptable for a no-show."

The voices in the car became hysterical.

"I was going to practice cheers with Linda after school and then go to the library."

"You know I have ball practice until 7."

"It seems to me I have a five o'clock dental appointment and traffic on the expressway is murder. Maybe Tuesday would be a better day."

"Well, if we're not finished loving one another by 6:30, I'm going to split."

I remained firm. "Dinner on Monday. Together."

On Monday at 6 P.M. the scene was set for the Great Spiritual banquet.

It held all the giddiness of the "Last Supper."

My husband had a mouthful of Novocaine and couldn't get his lips to cover his teeth.

One son appeared in stereo—a transistor in one ear and the phone in the other.

Our daughter had Linda waiting for her behind her chair.

And the other son dressed his arm in a sling to dispel the possibility of having to do dishes.

"Well now," I said, "now that we are all together, each one of us should think about sharing our day with one another. That should be an enriching experience."

"Do you know what Ramsey Phillips said were the seven words you can't use on TV?"

"Not that enriched," I said, clapping my hand over his mouth. "Dear," I said to my husband, "what would you like to talk about?"

237

That was a mistake.

Over the years, my husband has composed and committed to memory five standard dinner-table lectures that are as familiar to all of us as the Pledge of Allegiance. They include:

1. "WHY DON'T YOU WANT YOUR FATHER TO HAVE A LAWN?" (two minutes, forty seconds). This is a real heart-tugger in which Dad recaps his failure to triumph over bikes, sleds, plastic pools, football games, cars, wagons, dogs, and all the little perverts who cut across his lawn just to make him paranoid.

When his eyes begin to mist, he is ready to go for options. Donate the front yard to the government for nuclear testing. Put a sentry at the driveway with a loaded rifle. Or perhaps (and this is drastic) have the kids take an interest in mowing, fertilizing, and trimming the yard so they can appreciate what he is trying to do. His zinger is, "My compost is in your hands."

2. "DO I LOOK LIKE A MAN WHO OWNS THE WATER WORKS?" (one minute, forty-eight seconds).

This is a table favorite that is brought on when Dad is overcome by steam and requires oxygen when he tries to enter the bathroom. In his mind, he is convinced that he cannot afford the child who is trying to break into the Guinness Book of Records

for using forty gallons of hot water to wash off a ninety-six-pound body.

This is the lecture in which he uses visuals: prunes to show feet of child exposed to too many showers, and a broom illustrating how hair dries out and cracks from overshampooing. It's a two-parter, the second half taking place immediately following dinner when he takes the group to the bathroom and demonstrates how to turn off the faucet all the way.

3. "CAPTAIN QUEEG AND THE ICE CUBES" (one minute, thirty-four seconds). The children can always tell when Daddy is going for the Ice Cube number. He appears at the table with two steel balls in his hands and for five minutes does nothing but rotate them. Then he relates with a slight smile how he has trapped the culprit who put the ice cube tray in the freezer—*empty*. When he made his drink, there were nine ice cubes in the tray. By crouching unnoticed in the broom closet, he noted four of them were used by our daughter to make a malt, three were used by Mother for a glass of iced tea, and the younger son used one to suck on and he was the culprit.

When the younger son protested there was one left, his father's face lit up and he said. "Wrong! You dropped one on the floor to melt because I

slipped on it and nearly broke my back." The entire table is left to meditate on the consequences.

4. "I'M PAYING YOU KIDS AN ALLOWANCE TO BREATHE." (two minutes). This is a fun presentation because it's a group participation lecture.

"Do you know how much money I made when I was a child?" asks Daddy.

"Five cents a month," they yell in unison.

"Five cents a month," he says as if he hasn't heard them. "And do you know how old I was when I got my first car?"

"Twenty-three years old," they sigh.

"Twenty-three years old and do you know who bought it for me?"

"You did."

"I did," he says, "and have you any idea how much I had to buy with five cents a month?"

"You had to buy all your own clothes, books, tuition, medical expenses, rent, and pay for your entertainment."

"I had to buy all my own clothes, books, tuition, medical expenses, rent, and pay for my entertainment," he said. "And can you imagine what I did for entertainment?"

"Changed your underwear."

"Don't ad lib," he warns. "We really knew how to squeeze a buffalo in those days."

When three fourths of the table asks, "What's a buffalo, Daddy?" the lecture begins to deteriorate.

5. "I DON'T WANT TO TALK ABOUT IT" (thirty minutes). This is the lecture we have all come to dread. It's the I-Don't-Want-to-Talk-About-It lecture that he talks about all during dinner.

Dad appears at the table morose, depressed, and preoccupied, picking at his food—a picture of utter despair.

Finally, one of the kids will volunteer, "If it's about the duck in the utility room."

"I don't want to talk about it," he says.

"I'm going to empty all the garbage on the back porch tonight," promises another.

"Forget it," he says.

"Hey, just because your shorts came out pink doesn't mean we can't wash them again and put a little bleach . . ."

"It doesn't matter," he says tiredly.

By the end of the dinner hour, we have all confessed to every crime to date and he is still sullen.

Finally, in desperation, I say, "If it's about the dent in the car . . ."

"That's what I want to talk about," he says.

This Monday evening, however, my husband surprised us all by introducing a new lecture. It was called, "BY GOD, WE'RE GOING TO BE A CLOSE-

KNIT FAMILY IF I HAVE TO CHAIN YOU TO THE BED!"
He began:

"It certainly is wonderful sitting down to a table together for a change."

"Is that it?" asked our daughter, pushing back her chair. "Can I go now?"

"No!" he shouted. "We are going to sit here and get to know one another. I am your father."

"We thought you were taller," said the son with the sling on his arm.

"I'm sorry if I haven't seen as much of you as I would have liked. It isn't easy commuting to and from the city every day. Now, we are going to go around the table and each one of you can tell me something about yourself." He looked at our daughter.

"I'm the token girl in the family. I like birthday cards with money in them, bathroom doors that can't be unlocked from the outside by releasing it with a pin, and I want to be a professional cheerleader when I grow up. Can I go now or does it have to be longer?"

"Stay put," said her father. "Next," he said, turning to our son with his arm in a sling. "I'm the middle child in the family and am bored, depressed, neurotic, unfulfilled, and subject to pressures which will eventually drive me to my own apartment."

"Why not?" I said dryly. "You have to be driven everywhere else."

"Now, Mother," said Daddy, "it's not your turn."

"It's never my turn," I sulked. "Do you know what I think? I think you stopped loving me the day my upper arms became too big for puffed sleeves. Admit it?"

"Come now, let the boy talk."

"I have to do everything in this house," he continued. "Even though I was freed legally in 1860 by Lincoln. Take out the garbage. Let the dog out. Answer the phone. Get the paper. Change the channel on TV. Get Mom a drink of water."

"Drinking water wasn't my idea," I said wistfully.

"Hey, don't I get to say anything again?" asked the youngest. "Do you realize because I'm the baby of this family I never get to open my mouth. I've been trying to tell a joke at this table for the last three years."

Dad held up his hand for silence. "The boy is right. Take those wires out of your ears and tell us your joke."

"Well," he began, "there was this guy who stuttered a lot."

"I've heard it," said his brother, pushing away from the table.

"How do you know you've heard it? There are a lot of guys who stutter."

"I happen to know that of all the guys who stutter, only one of them made a joke out of it. Mom! Don't let him tell it. It's sick."

"It is not sick," persisted the youngest, "and was your stutterer from the South?"

"How long is this joke?" asked Linda, leaning over our daughter's shoulder. "If it's going to be much longer, I have to call home."

"You are excused to call your mother," said Dad. "Now continue with the joke."

"Well," he giggled, "this guy from the North said to the guy from the South, 'What are you doing up North?' And the stutterer said, 'Lllllooooook-kinnnng for a jjjob.' "

"Didn't I tell you it was sick? said his brother.

"Then," he continued, "his friend said, 'What sort of work are you looking for?' He said, 'Rrrrrrraaaaadddiooo aaannnouuunnnciing.' Then his friend asked, 'Any luck?' And this guy said (he held his sides with laughter as he blurted it out), 'Nnnnooo, whhhaaat chance does a sttttuutteerer have?' "

We all sat there in silence.

"That is the dumbest joke I've ever heard," said his sister.

244

"It's sick," said his brother.

"Are you sure you got the tagline right?" I asked.

"I've heard the joke," said his dad, "and the tagline is 'Whhat chaance hhhas a Soooutheeerner?'"

"Why is this family down on Southerners?" asked our daughter, leaving the table.

"I don't like your ending," said our youngest son.

"It's not *my* ending," said his father, "it's the way the joke goes."

"If you heard it before, you should have stopped me," he said, rushing to his room in tears.

"It's not my turn to do dishes," announced the last child, slipping out of his chair.

My husband turned to me. "When was the last spiritual family feast we shared together?"

"Four years ago at Grandma's birthday," I said numbly.

"Time flies when you're healing," he mused.

CHAPTER THIRTEEN

POSTSCRIPT TO SUBURBIAN GEMS

It was either Isaac Newton—or maybe it was Wayne Newton—who once said, "A septic tank does not last forever." He was right.

Suburbian Gems was a real community.

So were most of the characters in this book.

Certainly, the frustrations, the loneliness, the laughter, the challenges, and especially the analogy were for real. We were like pioneers, in a sense, leaving what we knew in search of our American dream.

Some settlers found Xanadu waiting in the suburbs. For others, it was an exile at San Clemente.

For me, it was one of the most exciting times of my life: a time when my children were young, my husband ambitious, and happiness for me was having a cake that didn't split in the middle and have to be rebuilt with toothpicks.

In the beginning, it was as we thought it would be: the smell of new wood (why not, it was green), doors that stuck permanently, and the weekend battle cry that shook the countryside, "Why pay someone to do it when we can do it ourselves."

The supermarket chains hadn't arrived yet with their frozen conveniences, express lines, and red lights over the pot roast.

There was only the country store where the owner was confused by the newcomers who insisted he bag the vegetables and ran him to his grain elevators for 15 cents' worth of pellets for a pet hamster.

I remember one Thanksgiving asking the kid at the gas pump in front of the store, "Do you have Mums?" he wiped his nose on his sleeve and said, "Yeah, but she's up at the house."

I never looked at the schools that I didn't imagine John Wayne saying to Beulah Bondi, "Someday this town is going to have a real school, and a school marm, and the children will learn to read and write their sums, etc. etc."

Our kids in the beginning got choked up when Spot chased a stick and Mommy put on a new apron. (Well, what did you expect from a twenty-year-old teacher who earned $1200 a year, taught five spelling classes, two history sessions, supervised the cafeteria during lunch, was class advisor for the Future Homemakers of America, and was in charge of the Senior class play and the drill team's peanut brittle candy sale.)

Later, that too changed when children would duly report to their parents, "I'm part of an innovative enrichment program that is structurally developed to stimulate my mental attitude with muscular development, combined with a language pattern design that is highly comprehensible and sensory." (One mother advised, "Keep your coat on, Durwood, and no one will notice.")

One book on the suburbs referred to it as "Creeping Suburbia." It sounded like a disease. ("This creeping suburbia has got me climbing the wall, Margaret.") Critics credit it with weakening the family structure, becoming overorganized, isolating people of like incomes, race, social levels, politics, religion, and attitudes from the rest of the world.

It probably did all of those things and some more that haven't been dissected and labeled yet.

But no one can quarrel with the unique sense of

belonging that got the suburban settlers involved in their communities.

In a few short years, it became one of the most powerful forces in this country. How they voted. How they ran their schools. How they designated their land. How they incorporated around them what they wanted and needed. How they were governed.

I only know that one morning I looked longingly beyond the suburbs to the city and said to my husband, "Got a letter from Marge and Ralph yesterday."

"When did they leave Pleasure Plantation for Crown City?"

"A week ago," I said. "Marge wrote, 'We reached the Downtown complex on the 15th. There are 17,500 units in our section, contained on 83 acres of land. There is rubble everywhere (they're still laying carpets in the hallways) and some of the elevators don't stop at our floor. None of the gift shops is open yet in the mall.' "

"The sheer guts of it," said my husband.

" 'The bus service to Ralph's office building in the suburbs is horrendous—sometimes every hour— sometimes an hour and fifteen minutes between buses. It's lonely and desolate here on the fifty-fifth floor. It's like floating in an atmosphere with no

trees, no birds . . . only the wind and an occasional jet.

" 'The children have to walk to school. It will take some getting used to after busing it in the suburbs, but they're becoming used to hardships. The mail deliveries, garbage pickups, fire and police protection are nonexistent, but the strike is expected to be settled as soon as the city is solvent again.

" 'There are some bright spots. No more getting in the car to go shopping. There is a store in the building that delivers and we are fortunate enough to have our own cloverleaf exit that comes directly into the building garage.

" 'Also, it is quiet. On a summer night we can walk and breathe clean air and feel no one else is around. Tomorrow, we are going to visit a tree. It is being planted in the mall in our building. Come visit us. You can't miss us. We have a lamp in the picture window.' "

I put the letter down. "Doesn't that sound exciting? Living in a city eighty stories high. That is where the next frontier is."

"What!" shouted my husband. "And give up all of this?"

I looked around. Our "wilderness" had grown to 100,000 people, fifteen traffic lights, five shopping centers, six elementary schools, two high schools,

fifteen churches, four drive-ins, a daily newspaper, and street lights on every corner.

Report cards were computerized, horses were "boarded," lube jobs on the car were "by appointment only" and there were three, sometimes four cars in every driveway.

Our garage bulged at the seams with lawn spreaders, leaf sweepers, automatic mowers, snow plows, golf carts, bob sleds, skis, ice skates, boats, and camping gear.

Our all-electric kitchen crackled with the efficiency of micro-ovens, dishwashers, ice cube crushers, slow-cooking pots, electric knife sharpeners, brooms, sanders, waxers, blenders, mixers, irons, and electric ice cream freezers and yogurt makers.

The once-silent streets had been replaced by motor and trail bikes, transistors, and piped-in music in the shopping-center parking lot and the air was thick with charcoal.

As we weighed our decision, I couldn't help but speculate how future historians would assess the suburbs—the ghost cities of tomorrow.

Poking through the rubble of that unique civilization, would they be able to figure out what 1200 bleacher seats and two goalposts were doing in the middle of a cornfield?

Would they be able to break the code of the neon signs that flapped in the wind: "GO-GO," "CARRY-OUT," "DRIVE-IN," or a sign that instructed, "SPEAK CLEARLY AND DIRECT YOUR ORDER INTO THE CLOWN'S MOUTH?"

Would they be dismayed by the impermanence of a Nova camper with a sign in the window, "SUNSET BANK. Hours: 8 A.M.–2 P.M. weekdays. CLOSED SATURDAYS AND SUNDAYS"?

Would they probe the sandboxes and come up with a Barbie and Ken form, and figure we got sick?

Or would they piece together scraps of PTA notices, home parties, church bazaars, and little Green Stamps (thirty to a page) and ponder, "How did they survive?"

At that moment the ghosts of 100 million settlers are bound to echo, "We drank!"

ABOUT THE AUTHOR

Erma Bombeck is the author of eight books: *At Wit's End;* *"Just Wait Till You Have Children of Your Own!"* (with Bil Keane); *I Lost Everything in the Post-Natal Depression;* and the bestsellers *The Grass Is Always Greener Over the Septic Tank; If Life Is a Bowl of Cherries—What Am I Doing in the Pits?; Aunt Erma's Cope Book; Motherhood: The Second Oldest Profession* and *Family: The Ties That Bind...and Gag!* Her thrice-weekly humor column, "At Wit's End," appears in 900 newspapers throughout the world and is read by an estimated 31 million people. Well known to television viewers, Erma was a regular on ABC's *Good Morning, America* for eleven years. She holds twelve honorary doctorates, was appointed to the President's Advisory Committee for Women, and has been named repeatedly to *The World Almanac*'s annual list of the 25 Most Influential Women in America. Erma and her husband, Bill, make their home in Paradise Valley, Arizona. They have three children.

My son was five years old when his teacher sent home a note informing me he was sexually immature.

I confronted her the next day after school and said, "What is this supposed to mean, Mrs. Kravitz?"

"It means we had a little quiz the other day on reproductive organs and he defined every one of them as an Askyourfather. You are sending a child into the world, Mrs. Bombeck, who thinks Masters and Johnson is a golf tournament and fertilization is something you do in the fall to make the lawns green."

"That's true," I nodded.

"Have you ever discussed sex in your home?" she asked.

"No, but once he caught Barbie and Ken together in a cardboard car in their underwear."

"Have you ever discussed with him the parts of his body?"

"Only those that showed dirt."

The Grass Is Always Greener Over The Septic Tank

Erma Bombeck

FAWCETT CREST • NEW YORK

P9-DZN-811